विज्ञानभैरव

Vijñānabhairava

or

Techniques for Entering Liminal Consciousness

Interpretation and notes
by Dmitri Semenov

January 2003 – June 2010

Sattarka Publications

ISBN 978-0-578-06042-2

To those who are vigorous
and
honest in their intentions.

Contents

Introduction 9
On practice 11
Scriptural sources 14
Acknowledgments 15
Techniques 17
Verse 24; Dh.1 29
Verse 25; Dh.2 31
Verse 26; Dh.3 32
Verse 27; Dh.4 33
Verse 28; Dh.5 34
Verse 29; Dh.6 35
Verse 30; Dh.7 37
Verse 31; Dh.8 39
Verse 32; Dh.9 40
Verse 33; Dh.10 41
Verse 34; Dh.11 42
Verse 35; Dh.12 43
Verse 36; Dh.13 44
Verse 37; Dh.14 45
Verse 38; Dh.15 46
Verse 39; Dh.16 47
Verse 40; Dh.17 49
Verse 41; Dh.18 50
Verse 42; Dh.19 51
Verse 43; Dh.20 52
Verse 44; Dh.21 53
Verse 45; Dh.22 54
Verse 46; Dh.23 55
Verse 47; Dh.24 56
Verse 48; Dh.25 57
Verse 49; Dh.26 58

Verse 50; Dh.27 59
Verse 51; Dh.28 60
Verse 52; Dh.29 61
Verse 53; Dh.30 62
Verse 54; Dh.31 63
Verse 55; Dh.32 65
Verse 56; Dh.33 69
Verse 57; Dh.34 70
Verse 58; Dh.35 71
Verse 59; Dh.36 72
Verse 60; Dh.37 73
Verse 61; Dh.38 74
Verse 62; Dh.39 75
Verse 63; Dh.40 76
Verse 64; Dh.41 77
Verse 65; Dh.42 78
Verse 66; Dh.43 79
Verse 67; Dh.44 80
Verse 68; Dh.45 81
Verse 69; Dh.46 82
Verse 70; Dh.47 83
Verse 71; Dh.48 84
Verse 72; Dh.49 85
Verse 73; Dh.50 86
Verse 74; Dh.51 87
Verse 75; Dh.52 88
Verse 76; Dh.53 89
Verse 77; Dh.54 90
Verse 78; Dh.55 92
Verse 79; Dh.56 93
Verse 80; Dh.57 94
Verse 81; Dh.58 95
Verse 82; Dh.59 96
Verse 83; Dh.60 97
Verse 84; Dh.61 98
Verse 85; Dh.62 99
Verse 86; Dh.63 100
Verse 87; Dh.64 101
Verse 88; Dh.65 102
Verse 89; Dh.66 103
Verse 90; Dh.67 104
Verse 91; Dh.68 105

Verse 92; Dh.69 106
Verse 93; Dh.70 107
Verse 94; Dh.71 108
Verse 95; Dh.72 109
Verse 96; Dh.73 111
Verse 97; Dh.74 112
Verse 98; Dh.75 113
Verse 99; Dh.76 114
Verse 100; Dh.77 115
Verse 101; Dh.78 116
Verse 102; Dh.79 117
Verse 103; Dh.80 118
Verse 104; Dh.81 119
Verse 105; Dh.82 120
Verse 106 121
Verse 107; Dh.83 122
Verse 108; Dh.84 123
Verse 109; Dh.85 124
Verse 110; Dh.86 125
Verse 111; Dh.87 126
Verse 112; Dh.88 127
Verse 113; Dh.89 128
Verse 114; Dh.90 129
Verse 115; Dh.91 130
Verse 116; Dh.92 131
Verse 117; Dh.93 132
Verse 118; Dh.94 133
Verse 119; Dh.95 134
Verse 120; Dh.96 135
Verse 121; Dh.97 136
Verse 122; Dh.98 137
Verse 123 138
Verse 124 138
Verse 125; Dh.99 139
Verse 126; Dh.100 142
Verse 127; Dh.101 143
Verse 128; Dh.102 144
Verse 129; Dh.103 145
Verse 130; Dh.104 146
Verse 131; Dh.105 147
Verse 132; Dh.106 148
Verse 133; Dh.107 149

Verse 134; Dh.108 150
Verse 135 151
Verse 136; Dh.109 152
Verse 137; Dh.110 153
Verse 138 154
Verses 139-141 155
Verses 142–143 156
Verses 144–145 157
Verses 146–147 159
Verses 148–149 160
Verses 150–151 161
Verses 152–153 162
Verses 154–155; Dh.111 163
Verse 156; Dh.112 164
Verses 157–160 165
Verses 161–163 167

Concepts **169**

Appendix **191**

Bibliography **194**

Index **194**

Introduction

From my earliest flashes of consciousness, I was tracking something that is beyond the grasp of ordinary language. Later I found that "something" is called "liberation" or "enlightenment", but words are not of much help in these matters. When wandering in nearly total darkness, one needs cairn-like landmarks, something intrinsic, in order to perceive the faint reflections of what can vaguely be called the "Self." Neither rituals, nor initiations, nor pontificating authority ever appealed to me. People who can understand on a practical level "I am the same Lord who becomes the Universe and dwells in its heart" were, and still are, somewhat of a mystery to me. To recognize the watchmaker, I needed to see the inner workings of the watch. To appease the spirits of Hellenic skepticism, I was looking for the precision of Aristotle and the non-presumptuousness of Socrates. I have found both the precision and the landmarks that allow one to regain this ground and orientation in the well developed philosophical system of Kashmir Shaivism.

Vijñānabhairava is an important scripture of Kashmir Shaivism and is devoted mostly to practical aspects of its monistic philosophy. It is one of the 64 tantras. The word *tantra*, in a narrow sense, means "a set of tools for the expansion of consciousness." Most of the 64 tantras seem to be lost, but among those surviving till modern times, *Vijñānabhairava* tantra is one of the most influential by the virtue of being the most flexible and applicable in the contexts of various philosophical systems of liberation.

This book is a translation of *Vijñānabhairava* and presents a collection of techniques for attaining a special state of consciousness — *bhairava*.

Literally, the word *bhairava* means "instilling terror, frightful." In practice, the state itself is tranquil, blissful, and serene. If one has strong attachments, the onset of this state might be quite terrifying in the same way freedom might be frightening to a prisoner who had spent twenty years chained to the wall of a small dark cell and was suddenly turned loose in a jungle. But the state of *bhairava* is to be experienced, not talked about.

Unlike many other texts, *Vijñānabhairava* puts the emphasis on the procedural aspect of the philosophical system it belongs to — Trika. Trika was formulated in the larger context of Kashmir Shaivism.[1]

No path is delineated in *Vijñānabhairava*, only improvisations at the point of the naked Unknown. Most such improvisations, though, should be carefully rehearsed before circumstances present an opportunity for actual practice.

Reading books on spiritual matters is sometimes similar to reading wine reviews. They are full of descriptions, such as "bright red, fruity, intertwined with a delicate mushroom-like character, with a long finish," but give no means to taste the wine. In this book the reader will find few descriptions of "how the spiritual experience feels and what it's like," but, rather, directions on how to experience it.

Many descriptions of the practices from *Vijñānabhairava* contain technical terms. These terms are defined in the chapter "Concepts," which begins on page 169.

The original Sanskrit text of *Vijñānabhairava* was written in verse. The style is peculiar, and I have tried to preserve it in my translation so that the very peculiarity might induce the mind to wander off its deep habitual tracks. No knowledge of Sanskrit is required to read this book.

Each verse is presented first in the original Devanagari,[2] followed by the same verse in Roman transliteration. There are many elliptical expressions in the verses, which have to be filled in order to understand the meaning of a sentence. When the translation includes extensive additions, these are put into square brackets []. Sanskrit words that are technical terms are given without any translation and in Roman transliteration. Following the translation is my commentary. In the table of contents a verse will have two numbers, one, the number of the verse in the text and the other, the number of the technique it describes. Traditionally the techniques are called *dhāraṇa* (an immovable concentration of the mind upon something) and are abbreviated as Dh.

---

[1]For a systematic exposition of this philosophical system, the reader is referred to [Sem08], [Sin00], [Lak00] and [Tor02].

[2]Devanagari is a syllabic script used in writing Sanskrit.

These typographic conventions look like this:

विज्ञानभैरव Original

Vijñānabhairava Transliteration

[Attaining the state of] Bhairava by means of discerning. Translation

---

Vijñānabhairava is the name of a tantra. It might be rendered as "Bhairava by Means of Discerning." Commentary

The translation is almost never literal, but interpretive. The interpretation relies heavily on my own personal experiences – those of a man – and, therefore, is limited by them. This implies the possibility that the versions of the techniques in this book will effect women differently – they might be less, more, or equally effective. To take into account gender differences in speech processing, social frames of reference, etc. will require substantial experimentation with the techniques. For some ideas in this direction see "The Book of Secrets" by Osho [Osh94] and "The Radiance Sutras" by Dr. Lorin Roche [LR08].

In addition to the mentioned above, there are at least four other notable interpretations of the *Vijñānabhairava* in English: by Jaideva Singh [Sin03b], by Swami Lakshman Joo [Joo02], by Satyasangananda Saraswati [Sar03], and by Daniel Odier [Odi05]. My understanding of this tantra was greatly enhanced by these works, and the reader is encouraged to become familiar with them as well. Differences in interpretations cannot be reconciled, in most cases, through linguistic or philosophical arguments — through direct experience one finds what works.

On practice

"If you don't know what to do, it is better not to do anything, because whatsoever you do without knowing is going to create more complexities than it can solve," wrote Osho in *The Book of Secrets*. Therefore, it is important to understand how the techniques work and to have some inner criteria for correctness.

The first step for obtaining such inner criteria might be just reading through all the techniques and recollecting if one has performed them in the past, however unconsciously or accidentally. Many techniques described here occur, in some form or another, naturally; they don't require any empowerment or initiation.

For example, upon reading this tantra, I recognized that since childhood I had been practicing several techniques without being aware of any tantras or even spirituality — simply to relieve the stress of the mind-numbing duality all around. One of those techniques was the *bhairavī-mudrā.* I would stand on the balcony of my family's apartment in Moscow and fixate my eyes on the buildings across the street, while consciously looking within. If I made no effort to see something in particular in those building, the visual picture would become more and more fragmentary and dim, to the point of disappearing. At that moment a deep peace would spread inside me. No one ever taught me this as a "technique," but I stumbled upon its description some 30 years later.

Upon recollecting previous occurrences of some of the techniques, one should look for any feelings of satiety, deep calm, lack of ego-induced boundaries, limitless spaciousness, or luminosity that might have accompanied such experiences. As you begin to practice the techniques, the similarity of sensations to these recollected raw impressions can be used as an initial criterion for correctness.

Some insight into how the techniques work can be gained from understanding the concepts behind the practices, as well as from verses 18–21.

This tantra offers no belief system, no ideology, and no religion. Instead, it offers the precision of a tool and the variety of a library to make one's chosen spiritual path closely interweave with the manifoldness of daily life. This scripture always gave me the opportunity to become aware of the deep inner currents of existence. It also never failed to give directions to further my individual yoga practice.

It is not necessary to practice all 112 techniques, rather, it is sufficient to learn 4–8 that work for you personally and provide ample opportunities to practice.

Most techniques are simple, and it is quite easy to experience the state of *bhairava* at least once in your practice. After that, the machinery of "individuality" will create obstacles to experiencing it again. Detecting the obstacles can be accomplished by introspection and through practicing several techniques, so that the obstacles become easier to spot by the virtue of coming at them from many angles.

Introspection as a tool of discovery is subject to extensive and valid critique. Nevertheless, introspection is of primary importance for practicing this tantra. But, to be a tool and not itself an obstacle, introspection must use a well developed language and set of analytical tools. Both are provided by the philosophical system of *Pratyabhijñahṛdaya*.

When one is searching for something true and throwing light onto the inner world, it is not that the doors of perception are cleansed, but that one looks at the ceiling and discovers that it is missing. This book gives ways to accomplish exactly this.

Among yoga practitioners, one often hears that it is all about "controlling the mind." How is the approach of this tantra, *Vijñānabhairava*, different? Controlling the mind is a temporary measure to prevent immediate harm. But it comes with long-term after-effects. It creates discontinuity between fountains of vitality and the controlling faculty. If impulses from these inner fountains are sealed from the heart of compassion and from the reasoning mind, then a practice becomes a progressively hallowed formality, shaped by mechanisms of social puppetry; or it becomes a duty, lacking inner meaning. At the same time, the vitality is channeled into the creation and nurturing of demons that dwell behind one's back. A more productive use of the temporary relief granted by controlling one's mind might be the unwinding or unraveling of those mental constructs, configurations of *tattva*-s, and so forth, that lead to the *necessity* of controlling one's mind in the first place. That is the way of tantra. The techniques of *Vijñānabhairava* lead to the creation of an inner space in which to do the unwinding, reconfigurations, etc. Instead of aiming at controlling the mind, this tantra is designed to take the opportunity of various states of the mind in order to advance a practitioner towards the ultimate goal.

Though it is stated in the verse 140 that mastering even *one* technique is enough to attain the ultimate goal, until one *masters* such a technique, one should practice at least four different techniques, each aiming to effect one of the following obstacles to entering the state of *bhairava*:

- mental dispositions;
- the urge and the faculty to weave explanations not warranted by facts;

- the energy that mediates between mental actions and physical actions;
- the energies of breath.

Verses on mental dispositions are: 32, 33, 41, 43–46, 58, 61, 62, 87, 94, 95, 97, 103, 121, 125, 126.

Verses on the urge and the faculty to weave explanations not warranted by facts are: 37, 38, 50, 53, 66, 101, 122, 134.

Verses on the energy that mediates between mental actions and physical actions are: 29–31, 36, 39, 80, 83, 93, 104, 113.

Verses on the energies of breath are: 24–28, 64, 67, 154–156.

Other verses are either more integral or have no specificity to any one obstacle type.

The general attitude towards the practices should be playfulness. That, according to Kashmir Shaivism, is the true spirit of this Universe.

Scriptural sources

Here are scriptural sources used and abbreviations for them.

TA	*Tantrāloka* by Abhinavagupta
AbhTs	*Tantrasāra* by Abhinavagupta
IPK	*Īśvarapratyabhijñākārikā* by Utpaladeva
ShS	*Śivasūtra*
ShSv	*Śivasvarodaya*
PH	*Pratyabhijñāhṛdayam*
VBh	*Vijñānabhairava*
BhG	*Bhagavadgītā*
YS	*Yogasūtra* by Patanjali
HYP	*Haṭhayogapradīpika* by Svatmarama
MrA	*Mṛgendrāgama*
ManUp	*Māṇḍukyopaniṣad*

Acknowledgments

Special thanks to Shae Isaacs who undertook the hard work of editing the draft of the book.

Techniques

This tantra, like a few others, is written in the form of a dialog between *Śiva*, represented as the male deity, and *Śakti*, represented as the female deity, although as the verse 10 says, these symbolic devices are "only for the sake of mental representation, for those who have confused notions and for those engaged in the ostentatious performance of rituals."

At the beginning of the dialog, *Śakti* is emerging from *Śiva*'s throat. She merges back into it at the end of the dialog. Upon emerging, *Śakti* has a variety of questions to ask. *Śiva* proceeds to answer these questions, though *Śakti* is not separate, in the ultimate sense, from him, but is his inherent emanation. So it appears that *Śiva* is talking to himself.

One of the meanings of this parable is that an emergence of an instance of speech is a moment of bifurcation, of conditioned duality, that brings an apparent ignorance by obfuscating inherent knowledge. The bifurcation results in a blooming, multidimensional manifestation that carries the duality "that which is a symbol of itself only" vs. "utterance, having a primarily conventional link to *this* by means of opposition to *that*" into all of its aspects. Despite the obfuscation, correct speech, pointing at particular knowledge, shows a path to the knowledge that became hidden through the emergence of speech. Once the hidden becomes self-evident, then the apparent duality retracts into that undifferentiated Luminous Void denoted with the word *Śiva*.

This tantra has quite a few (112 to be exact) practices, or techniques. An important point to keep in mind is that the techniques do not create, or cause, the state of *bhairava*. They merely lead to an extensive indeterminacy, which is on the verge of that state. This final transition cannot be forced or conditioned, but occurs spontaneously and unpredictably. This point is reflected in the text by the variety of descriptions of the places to which the techniques lead a practitioner. For example, verse 36 describes the state attained by its technique as "the ultimate stillness," verse 39 says that "one goes towards the voidness," verse 51 describes it as "ever increasing indefiniteness," while verse 64 puts it as "the simultaneous arising of the discerning and of the equanimity," etc. All of these descriptions point at states that are bordering the state of *bhairava*, which itself is not subject to direct description.

What happens as a direct result of these practices is called *vijñāna*, or "discerning". So, the title of this tantra, *Vijñānabhairava*, might be rendered as "Bhairava by Means of Discerning," keeping in mind that "discerning" is a technical term. *Vijñāna* is an etching into the perceptive field through an accumulation of subliminal impressions. It happens the same way the style of a particular painter becomes etched into perception, so that one is able to "recognize" a never seen before painting as likely to be by the same artist. It is hardly possible to point at and verbalize what that style is and how it is different from other artists' styles, but it is still possible to "recognize" an artist's work that way. The practices, described on pages 29–164, all aim at this "etching" of a particular mental dynamic that is a transition to the state of *bhairava* from the liminal states bordering it. After a while, such transitions become easier to trigger and require less effort to be a result of a practice.

The structure of the original text is as follows:

- introduction, in which questions are asked; verses 1–23 (pages 19–28);
- list of techniques, leading to the state of *bhairava*; verses 24–137, 154–156 (pages 29–153, 163–164);
- philosophical points, important for practice; verses 138–153 (pages 154–162);
- final remarks on the transmission of the teaching; verses 157–163 (pages 165–167).

Throughout the text, both *Śiva* and *Śakti* have many names.

Names used for *Śiva* are *Bhairava*, *Deva* (God), *Parameśvara* (Highest Lord), *Maheśvara* (Great Lord), *Nātha* (Protector), *Parambrahma* (Ultimate Brahma).

Names used for *Śakti* are *Bhairavī*, *Devī* (Goddess), *Mahādevī* (Great Goddess), *Mṛgekṣaṇā* (Gazelle-eyed).

श्रीदेव्युवाच ।

śrīdevyuvāca

Devī said:

In verses 1–6 *Devī* is asking *Deva* some questions.

श्रुतं देव मया सर्वं रुद्रयामलसम्भवम् ।
त्रिकभेदमशेषेण सारात्सारविभागशः ॥ १॥

śrutaṃ deva mayā sarvaṃ rudrayāmalasambhavam |
trikabhedam aśeṣeṇa sārāt sāravibhāgaśaḥ || 1||

O *Deva*, I've heard everything contained in the *Rudrayāmala* tantra, the entire classification by triads, from the very core to the peripheral details.

The *Rudrayāmala* tantra is a text that is not currently available. Many existing scriptures cite it as an authoritative source for other tantras and teachings.

अद्यापि न निवृत्तो मे संशयः परमेश्वर ।
किं रूपं तत्त्वतो देव शब्दराशिकलामयम् ॥ २॥

adyāpi na nivṛtto me saṃśayaḥ parameśvara |
kiṃ rūpaṃ tattvato deva śabdarāśikalāmayam || 2||

To this day, though, the uncertainty did not not recede for me, O *Parameśvara*! O *Deva*, in reality, what form consists of the multitude of sounds?

This reference to "the multitude of sounds" is explained by the following verse from the third book of Tantraloka:

> *ekāmarśasvabhāvatve śabdarāśiḥ sa bhairavaḥ |*
> *āmṛśyacchāyayā yogātsaiva śaktiśca mātṛkā || 198||.*
>
> "When in the natural state of single-pointed awareness, *bhairava* is the multitude of sounds. Having reflected [upon himself], and in consequence of this reflection, he becomes *śakti* and the alphabet."

The alphabet here means the organized set of all Sanskrit letters, where each letter has sound, function, and meaning. Letters in this conceptual system are the building blocks of phonetics, syntax, and semantics.

किं वा नवात्मभेदेन भैरवे भैरवाकृतौ ।
त्रिशिरोभेदभिन्नं वा किं वा शक्तित्रयात्मकम् ॥ ३॥

kiṃ vā navātmabhedena bhairave bhairavākṛtau |
triśirobhedabhinnaṃ vā kiṃ vā śaktitrayātmakam || 3||

Is [that form] divided into parts by the divergence of the three tendencies, or because of the divergence into the nine layers in the *bhairava* [state itself], or in the aspects of the *bhairava* state? Or, is it just a composite of the three *śakti*-s?

The three *śakti*-s mentioned are *jñāna-śakti*, *kriyā-śakti*, and *icchā-śakti*, which can be translated approximately as the ability to perceive and to know, the ability to act, and the ability to desire, respectively (see entries in the "Concepts" chapter for details). This is the basic triad of the Trika system. It is projected onto many concepts and phenomena. In some modern psychological theories, *jñāna-śakti* is subdivided into the ability to perceive and into the ability to know.

The nine layers mentioned are the nine sub-diagrams of the mystical diagram (or *yantra*) called *Śrī Cakra*.

नादबिन्दुमयं वापि किं चन्द्रार्धनिरोधिकाः ।
चक्रारूढमनच्कं वा किं वा शक्तिस्वरूपकम् ॥ ४॥

nādabindumayaṃ vāpi kiṃ candrārdhanirodhikāḥ |
cakrārūḍhamanackaṃ vā kiṃ vā śaktisvarūpakam || *4* ||

Does it consist of the nasalization of sounds which becomes *candrārdha*, *nirodhika*, etc.?[3] Is it the humming sound, spreading through *suṣumnā*, or is it just a quality of *śakti*?

परापरायाः सकलमपरायाश्च वा पुनः ।
पराया यदि तद्वत्स्यात्परत्वं तद्विरुध्यते ॥ ५॥
न हि वर्णविभेदेन देहभेदेन वा भवेत् ।
परत्वं निष्कलत्वेन सकलत्वे न तद्भवेत् ॥ ६॥

parāparāyāḥ sakalamaparāyāśca vā punaḥ |
parāyā yadi tadvatsyātparatvaṃ tadvirudhyate || *5* ||
na hi varṇavibhedena dehabhedena vā bhavet |
paratvaṃ niṣkalatvena sakalatve na tadbhavet || *6* ||

If *śakti* in the *parā* state were to have any separate parts, as it does in the *parā-aparā* and *aparā* states, then that quality of "being ultimate" would be limited by them.

She cannot become *parā-aparā* and *aparā* through a divergence into phonemes nor through divergence into different shapes, because ultimateness, by being devoid of constituent parts, cannot exist in a composite.

[3] These are various degrees of the nasalization of a vowel before consonants.

प्रसादं कुरु मे नाथ निःशेषं छिन्द्धि संशयम् ।

prasādaṃ kuru me nātha niḥśeṣaṃ chinddhi saṃśayam |

O *Nātha*, do me a favor, remove completely this uncertainty!

भैरव उवाच ।

bhairava uvāca |

Bhairava said:

साधु साधु त्वया पृष्टं तन्त्रसारमिदम् प्रिये ॥ ७॥

sādhu sādhu tvayā pṛṣṭaṃ tantrasāramidam priye || *7*||

Well, well! Here it is, the very essence of tantra you demanded to know, O Dear!

In verses 8–13, *Deva* explains what *bhairava* is not.

गूहनीयतमं भद्रे तथापि कथयामि ते ।
यत्किंचित्सकलं रूपं भैरवस्य प्रकीर्तितम् ॥ ८॥

gūhanīyatamaṃ bhadre tathāpi kathayāmi te |
yatkiṃcitsakalaṃ rūpaṃ bhairavasya prakīrtitam || *8*||

Though it should be kept as the utmost secret, my good Lady, I will, nevertheless, describe for you whatever composite form of *bhairava* mentioned [in the *Rudrayāmala* tantra] that can be represented with words.

तदसारतया देवि विज्ञेयं शक्रजालवत् ।
मायास्वप्नोपमं चैव गन्धर्वनगरभ्रमम् ॥ ९॥
ध्यानार्थं भ्रान्तबुद्धीनां क्रियाडम्बरवर्तिनाम् ।
केवलं वर्णितम् पुंसां विकल्पनिहतात्मनाम् ॥ १०॥

tadasāratayā devi vijñeyaṃ śakrajālavat |
māyāsvapnopamaṃ caiva gandharvanagarabhramam || 9||
dhyānārthaṃ bhrāntabuddhīnāṃ kriyāḍambaravartinām |
kevalaṃ varṇitam puṃsāṃ vikalpanihatātmanām || 10||

O *Devī*, each such description has to be regarded, because of its fragility, as illusory, as having a semblance of a dream or an apparition, or as a shimmering mirage of a town in the sky,[4] solely depicted for the sake of mental representation for those who have confused notions and for those engaged in the ostentatious performance of rituals, [and for those] men whose Self is struck down by an antithesis[5] of opposites.

तत्त्वतो न नवात्मासौ शब्दराशिर् न भैरवः ।
न चासौ त्रिशिरा देवो न च शक्तित्रयात्मकः ॥ ११॥
नादबिन्दुमयो वापि न चन्द्रार्धनिरोधिकाः ।
न चक्रक्रमसम्भिन्नो न च शक्तिस्वरूपकः ॥ १२॥

tattvato na navātmāsau śabdarāśir na bhairavaḥ |
na cāsau triśirā devo na ca śaktitrayātmakaḥ || 11||
nādabindumayo vāpi na candrārdhanirodhikāḥ |
na cakrakramasambhinno na ca śaktisvarūpakaḥ || 12||

In reality, it[6] does not have nine layers; the multitude of speech sounds is not *bhairava*, and it is not the three-headed deity, and it cannot not be reduced to the triad of *śakti*-s.[7]

---

[4]Fata Morgana, created by the great magician — the language.
[5]See entry *vikalpa* in "Concepts" chapter.
[6]*bhairava*.
[7]See commentary to verse 3.

[It does not consist] of nasalization of sounds, nor [is it] *candrārdha*, *nirodhika*, etc.[8]

[It cannot be] made completely disjoint by the sequential penetration of *cakra*-s[9] [during arising of the humming sound in the *suṣumnā*], and it is not just a quality of *śakti.*

अप्रबुद्धमतीनां हि एता बलविभीषिकाः ।
मातृमोदकवत्सर्वं प्रवृत्त्यर्थं उदाहृतम् ॥ १३॥

aprabuddhamatīnāṃ hi etā balavibhīṣikāḥ |
mātṛmodakavatsarvaṃ pravṛttyarthaṃ udāhṛtam || 13||

Though all these (*candrārdhā*, *nirodhikā*, etc.) are effective means to scare away those whose thoughts lack awareness, it was said that for those who intend on advancing, the ideas are exhilarating like a mother.

In verses 14 through 21, the principle behind all practical techniques of this tantra is described.

दिक्कालकलनोन्मुक्ता देशोद्देशाविशेषिनी ।
व्यपदेष्टुमशक्यासावकथ्या परमार्थतः ॥ १४॥

dikkālakalanonmuktā deśoddeśāviśeṣinī |
vyapadeṣṭumaśakyāsāvakathyā paramārthataḥ || 14||

When deprived of opportunities to effect [the sense of] direction [in the subtle body] or of moments of time [in the mind], or when characterized by the absence of any particular location or exemplification, *śakti* is impossible to represent [using something else] and she is not describable, in the ultimate sense, with words.

---

[8] Various degrees of nasalization of a vowel before consonants.
[9] See Appendix.

अन्तः स्वानुभवानन्दा विकल्पोन्मुक्तगोचरा ।
यावस्था भरिताकारा भैरवी भैरवात्मनः ॥ १५॥

antaḥ svānubhavānandā vikalponmuktagocarā |
yāvasthā bharitākārā bhairavī bhairavātmanaḥ || 15||

That inner condition that is full of the bliss of self-perception [inherent in the self-will], that produces a sense of satiety, and which is attainable by those who set aside polarizations[10] is a quality of *Bhairava* called *Bhairavī.*

When strong polarizations exist, they channel the energy of arising *śakti* into activity controlled by these polarizations. This dissipation of energy results in a lack of satiety, or fullness, and in the disruption of self-perception, since only one extreme of any polarization is included into "self." This disruption inhibits the experience of the bliss inherent in *śiva.*

तद्वपुस्तत्त्वतो ज्ञेयं विमलं विश्वपूरणम् ।
एवं विधे परे तत्त्वे कः पूज्यः कश् च तृप्यति ॥ १६॥

tadvapustattvato jñeyaṃ vimalaṃ viśvapūraṇam |
evaṃ vidhe pare tattve kaḥ pūjyaḥ kaś ca tṛpyati || 16||

That [other] state[11] really should be known as devoid of the fault-causing conditions[12] and as making everything whole.

So, there are these two aspects, two ultimate *tattva*-s; which is to be worshiped and which satisfies?

एवं विधा भैरवस्य यावस्था परिगीयते ।
सा परापररूपेण परा देवी प्रकीर्तिता ॥ १७॥

[10]See entry *vikalpa* in "Concepts" chapter
[11]The state of *bhairava.*
[12]See entry *mala* in "Concepts" chapter.

evaṃ vidhā bhairavasya yāvasthā parigīyate |
sā parāpararūpeṇa parā devī prakīrtitā || 17||

Verily, the *bhairava* aspect is the state which is lauded most, while she, *parā-śakti*, in the *parā-apara* form, [is just] mentioned.

शक्तिशक्तिमतोर्यद्वदभेदः सर्वदा स्थितः ।
अतस्तद्धर्मधर्मित्वात् पराशक्तिः परात्मनः ॥ १८ ॥

śaktiśaktimatoryadvadabhedaḥ sarvadā sthitaḥ |
atastaddharmadharmitvāt parāśaktiḥ parātmanaḥ || 18||

Since that which lacks a division into a potency and that which possesses that potency is always invariable [or self-identical], therefore *parā-śakti* is made non-distinct from *śiva* [by dissolving into him], through being endowed with any attribute that promotes her stability [and thus prevents *parā-śakti* from evolving into manifoldness by assuming the *apāra* form].

The idea is to make expressions of *śakti* static and invariable, and thus, to make her merge back into the stillness of *śiva* by becoming non-distinct from him.

न वह्नेर्दाहिका शक्तिर्व्यतिरिक्ता विभाव्यते ।
केवलं ज्ञानसत्तायां प्रारम्भोऽयम् प्रवेशने ॥ १९ ॥
शक्त्यवस्था प्रविष्टस्य निर्विभागेन भावना ।
तदासौ शिवरूपी स्यात्शैवी मुखमिहोच्यते ॥ २० ॥

na vahnerdāhikā śaktirvyatiriktā vibhāvyate |
kevalaṃ jñānasattāyāṃ prārambho'yam praveśane || 19||
śaktyavasthā praviṣṭasya nirvibhāgena bhāvanā |
tadāsau śivarūpī syātśaivī mukhamihocyate || 20||

The ability of fire to burn is not made to appear as remaining after the fire is gone. But in reality, the experience of fire is such only in the beginning of moving [one's hand] into the flames. When one keeps the hand in the fire long enough, the condition *śakti* is in is that of realization, of forming a concept of the fire's ability to burn, which remains after the fire is gone.

A similar condition of *śakti*, manifesting as a blissful tranquility, can become a realization of the state of *bhairava*. In such a case the condition is called "*śiva*'s face."

See the verse 101 for a technique directly based on this principle.

यथालोकेन दीपस्य किरणैर्भास्करस्य च ।
ज्ञायते दिग्विभागादि तद्वच्छक्त्या शिवः प्रिये ॥ २१ ॥

yathālokena dīpasya kiraṇairbhāskarasya ca |
jñāyate digvibhāgādi tadvacchaktyā śivaḥ priye || 21 ||

Just as directions in space, etc. are made known by a spot of light produced by a lamp or by rays of sun, likewise *śiva* [is made known] by [expressions of] *śakti* , O Dear!

Thus, the general principle behind all practical techniques of *Vijñānabhairava* tantra is this:

When śakti is in the parā-aparā state, which has the potential for a blissful tranquility, prevent her from transitioning into an aparā state; make her static, as if immutable; and maintain this static character for a sufficiently long time. The resulting parā state of śakti will reveal the state of bhairava.

श्री देव्युवाच ।

śrī devyuvāca |

Devī said:

देव देव त्रिशूलाण्क कपालकृतभूषण ।
दिग्देशकालशून्या च व्यपदेशविवर्जिता ।
यावस्था भरिताकारा भैरवस्योपलभ्यते ॥ २२॥
कैरुपायैर्मुखं तस्य परा देवी कथंभवेत् ।
यथा सम्यगहं वेद्मि तथा मे ब्रूहि भैरव ॥ २३॥

deva deva triśūlāṇka kapālakṛtabhūṣaṇa |
digdeśakālaśūnyā ca vyapadeśavivarjitā |
yāvasthā bharitākārā bhairavasyopalabhyate || *22*||
kairupāyairmukhaṃ tasya parā devī kathaṃbhavet |
yathā samyagahaṃ vedmi tathā me brūhi bhairava || *23*||

O *Deva*, whose sign is the trident and who is adorned with skulls! Which condition of *śakti*, devoid of direction, space, and time, and stripped of all representations that expose the completeness and satiety [of *śiva*], is capable of revealing the state of *bhairava*?

And by what means, and how, could *parā-śakti* become *śiva*'s face?

In whatever manner I would understand it correctly, in such manner explain it to me, O *Bhairava*!

भैरव उवाच ।

bhairava uvāca |

Bhairava said:

Verses 24–156 are dedicated to the description of concrete techniques that lead to the realization of *bhairava*.

ऊर्ध्वे प्राणो ह्यधो जीवो विसर्गात्मा परोच्चरेत् ।
उत्पत्तिद्वितयस्थाने भरणाद्भरिता स्थितिः ॥ २४ ॥

ūrdhve prāṇo hyadho jīvo visargātmā paroccaret |
utpattidvitayasthāne bharaṇādbharitā sthitiḥ || *24* ||

If *śakti* were to arise in the *parā* state as having the nature of *vis-* Dh. 1
arga, [when] *prāṇa* is in the upper region and *apāna* in the lower, and instead of producing the two [flows separately, *śakti* were to become manifested as one state], then, from maintaining [this state by cessation of breathing], she who produces the sense of satiety would become static [and makes thus the state of *bhairava* manifest].

Exhale, using the diaphragm. Somewhere around the middle of your exhalation, start inhaling with the mouth and/or nose. Notice that the breathing stops when both inhalation and exhalation are about the same strength. If no intentional obstructions to either *prāṇa* or *apāna* are present, they will collide, creating tense stillness. If there is no anxiety to get rid of this tension and no mental activity attempting to comprehend or introspect into it, then, holding full attention on this stillness, even for a moment, will set in a transition to greater stillness. If holding the breath becomes difficult, breath again, and then repeat the superimposition just described. After 10–15 such repetitions, the transition into undifferentiated, featureless stillness will become as if etched into consciousness; there will be a change, ever so subtle but luminous, in the state of conscious awareness.

Visarga is a sound that is like an echo of the preceding vowel. It is pronounced by moving the tongue to utter *s* after the vowel, but relaxing the tongue before it touches the place where *s* would have been pronounced. The movement of tongue downwards results in air moving into the mouth, as if one is starting to inhale with open mouth. The superimposition of two movements here — inhalation and exhalation — is analogous to that of uttering a *visarga*.

Swami Lakshman Joo says that this practice consists of exhaling while pronouncing silently *saḥ* and placing *manas* into external *dvādaśānta*; then inhaling while pronouncing silently *haṃ* and placing *manas* into the *anāhata-cakra.*[13] In this way the *mantra so'haṃ* is articulated. Here the expression "silent pronouncing" means "configuring the voice apparatus as if uttering the sound, but keeping the tension low so that air might pass without producing the sound."

Jaideva Singh adds yet another interpretation of this practice that yields the same result: inhale while silently pronouncing *ha*; exhale with *saḥ*; at the junction between the end of inhalation and the beginning of exhalation, silently articulate the sound *ṃ*. The attention should be shifting so that it is on the *anāhata-cakra* at the start of *ha* and in the *dvādaśānta* at the start of *saḥ*. In this way the *mantra haṃsaḥ* is articulated.

The *dvādaśānta* mentioned is the point twelve thumb-widths above the top of the skull. The *anāhata-cakra* is in the center of the upper body, right between the two nipples.

s is pronounced as the English *s* in *sun*, *h* is pronounced as the English *h* in *hut*, *a* is pronounced as the English vowel in *sun*, *ḥ* denotes *visarga* (how to pronounce it is explained above). *ṃ* is a nasal sound that is like a humming vibration when air goes out through the nasal cavity while the mouth is slightly open.

[13]See Appendix.

मरुतोऽन्तर्बहिर्वापि वियद्युग्मानिवर्तनात् ।
भैरव्या भैरवस्येत्थं भैरवि व्यज्यते वपुः ॥ २५॥

maruto'ntarbahirvāpi viyadyugmānivartanāt |
bhairavyā bhairavasyettham̩ bhairavi vyajyate vapuḥ || *25*||

O *Bhairavī*, through uninterrupted transitions, whether of coming Dh. 2
together or of going apart, of breaths, either internally [that is, when breathing in turns into breathing out] or externally [that is, when breathing out turns into breathing in], the state of *bhairava* is etched by *śakti* [into the conscious awareness].

Observe how a subtle tension, causing to inhale, develops throughout an inhalation. Similarly, observe how a subtle tension, causing to exhale, develops throughout an exhalation. When an inhalation ends and an exhalation starts, there is a gap between fading of one tension and arising of another. If one maintains the flow of tension that is causing an inhalation, so that it overlaps the tension, that is causing the flow of exhalation, then there is no internal gap. Similarly, if the tension causing exhalation is extended beyond the start of inhalation, then there will be no external gap. In both cases one should try to avoid gap-like changes in attention focus, making all transitions as smooth as possible. These overlapping flows of exhalation and inhalation, along with the steady attention, will remove obstacles to the predominance of the state of *bhairava*.

Another interpretation, given by Jaideva Singh, is to simply maintain unwavering attention on each of the gaps, observing them. The difficulty of such an observation is that a transition between an inhalation and an exhalation causes attention to "flicker." By repeatedly maintaining observing attention and avoiding the "flickering," one gets to the verge of the state of *bhairava*.

न व्रजेन्न विशेच्छक्तिर्मरुद्रूपा विकासिते ।
निर्विकल्पतया मध्ये तया भैरवरूपता ॥ २६ ॥

na vrajenna viśecchaktirmarudrūpā vikāsite |
nirvikalpatayā madhye tayā bhairavarūpatā || *26* ||

Dh. 3 If *śakti*, in the form of breath, is in the state when an inhalation has ended but the next exhalation has not started, or is in the state when an exhalation has ended but the next inhalation has not started, then she assumes the state of *bhairava* in the middle channel and is caused to expand by the absence of the [inhale/exhale] polarization.

This practice is related to the gap between inhalation and exhalation, but in a way that is somewhat opposite of the previous verse. Instead of causing overlap between the two flows, this technique aims at creating a pause when neither flow exists. It requires knowledge of *prāṇāyāma* and the ability to refrain from breathing, both in muscular action and intention. At such cessation of breathing, one just allows attention to dwell in the middle channel (*suṣumnā*). Everything else happens by itself.

कुम्भिता रेचिता वापि पूरिता वा यदा भवेत् ।
तदन्ते शान्तनामासौ शक्त्या शान्तः प्रकाशते ॥ २७॥

kumbhitā recitā vāpi pūritā vā yadā bhavet |
tadante śāntanāmāsau śaktyā śāntaḥ prakāśate || 27||

Whenever *śakti* of the breath is rendered ineffective during suspension of breathing, either after inhalation or after exhalation, then the tranquility [of *bhairava* form] manifests itself through this extinguished state of *śakti*. Dh. 4

If, after an exhalation is over, the urge to inhale is prevented from resulting in inhalation or in any muscular tension, then the energy of that urge, when the urge becomes lower than a certain level, dissolves as if into a void. In this dissolution the state of *bhairava* sets in. The attention during this process should be focused on the urge, and all muscular tension should be relaxed as soon as it appears.

Follow the same practice for the suspension of breath after an inhalation is over and before the exhalation starts.

आ मूलात्किरणाभासां सूक्ष्मात्सूक्ष्मतरात्मिकाम् ।
चिन्तयेत्तां द्विषट्कान्ते शाम्यन्तीं भैरवोदयः ॥ २८ ॥

ā mūlātkiraṇābhāsāṃ sūkṣmātsūkṣmatarātmikām |
cintayettāṃ dviṣaṭkānte śāmyantīṃ bhairavodayaḥ || 28||

Dh. 5 If one turns attention to the *śakti* of the breath when she is still at the level of intent to breathe in, as a beam of light rising from *mūladhāra-cakra*[14] and being extinguished, allayed at the edge of twelve [thumb-widths above the top of the skull], then the arising of the *bhairava* state [occurs].

The spine should be straight. At the end of a deep exhalation, with the mind relaxed and worry free, observe inside the body, about five thumb-widths below the navel, a "thickening" of the intent to start inhalation. At that point in time, imagine a beam of light, arising from *mūladhāra-cakra*. Let this light be like the first rays of sun at dawn, following a sleepless night in the cold outdoors. As the tension of the intent builds up, visualize this beam reaching up the spine as high as twelve thumb-widths above the top of the skull and dissolving there into nothing, in the same way a beam of light, falling from a high window in a cathedral, disappears into the darkness of empty air. This visualization is transmuting the intent to inhale into the brightness of the light, and thus the breathing is stopped. If the urge to breathe becomes distracting from the visualization, one should inhale and breathe freely until the breath is relaxed; then try again ... and again. The successive periods of effective visualization accumulate, tuning the mind into the state of spacious tranquility.

[14]See Appendix.

उद्गच्छन्तीं तडित्रूपांप्रतिचक्रं क्रमात्क्रमम् ।
ऊर्ध्वं मुष्टित्रयं यावत्तावदन्ते महोदयः ॥ २९ ॥

udgacchantīṃ taḍitrūpāṃpraticakraṃ kramātkramam |
ūrdhvaṃ muṣṭitrayaṃ yāvattāvadante mahodayaḥ || *29*||

If one were to visualize her, *śakti*, as lightning, originating in the *mūladhāra-cakra*[15] and going upwards, piercing in turn each *cakra*, and reaching as far as three widths of one's fist above the top of skull, then the arising of the great [state of *bhairava* would occur]. Dh. 6

Start by creating tension in *mūladhāra-cakra*. This can be created by "breathing into it." That's how it's done. During inhalation (that is, when the diaphragm moves down), feel how subtle energy flows from outside space into the *mūladhāra-cakra*; during exhalation (that is, when the diaphragm relaxes upwards), feel how the energy is pushed out of the body through the *mūladhāra-cakra*. Several cycles of breath will create the required tension.

As soon as tension arises in *mūladhāra-cakra*, let it discharge, as if it were a flash of lightning into the next *cakra* (*svādhiṣṭhāna-cakra*). The discharge is attained by keeping the focus of attention primarily on the next *cakra*, while keeping the tension in the *mūladhāra-cakra* in the scope of attention. Be careful not to attempt to direct the tension from one *cakra* to the next by means of visualization with the help of volition: the transfer of the tension should happen by itself, spontaneously, as if lightning were striking ground — one can watch it, but cannot influence how and when it happens. Similarly, one should not try to control the transfer of the tension. Follow the same process for the discharge from *svādhiṣṭhāna-cakra* into *maṇipūra-cakra*, but keep the tension originating in the *mūladhāra-cakra* in the scope of attention. Then, similarly, make the transfer into the next *cakra*, piercing all intermediate *cakra*-s in turn. The last discharge is from *sahasrāra-cakra* into the spot twelve thumb-widths above the top of the skull. Maintain this last stage (when *śakti* discharges into the spot above the head) for several minutes, while maintaining the arising of tension in the *mūladhāra-cakra* by means of "breathing into it" and the

[15] See Appendix.

subsequent discharge of the tension through intermediate *cakra*-s, as described above.

All *cakra*-s visualized as pierced should be open (one will need to practice additional techniques to attain this openness), but try this technique even if you are not sure all *cakra*-s are indeed open.

क्रमद्वादशकं सम्यग्द्वादशाक्षरभेदितम् ।
स्थूलसूक्ष्मपरस्थित्या मुक्त्वा मुक्त्वान्ततः शिवः ॥ ३० ॥

kramadvādaśakaṃ samyagdvādaśākṣarabheditam |
sthūlasūkṣmaparasthityā muktvā muktvāntataḥ śivaḥ || *30* ||

Having loosened [the boundaries between] the sequential dozen, clearly differentiated into twelve vowels [in the beginning], by maintaining gross–subtle–ultimate [order of recitation], one finally becomes liberated [from them], and thus becomes *śiva*. Dh. 7

The "sequential dozen" is the list of twelve Sanskrit vowel sounds: *a ā i ī u ū e ai o au aṃ aḥ*.

The practice consists of reciting them in a particular fashion.

First, they should be recited aloud with distinct and clear articulation, from *a* to *aḥ*. This is the gross level of recitation.

Next, they should be recited silently, from *a* to *aḥ*. Silent recitation happens when the tensions of the voice apparatus required to articulate each sound are only indicated, but no audible sound results from the activity. Throat, tongue, and voice chords indicate moves and tensions, but of insufficient strength to produce a sound. This is the subtle level of recitation. During it, separations between articulations are less pronounced than they are during voiced recitation.

Lastly, the same sequence of vowel sounds should be recited on the purely intentional level; no voice apparatus muscles are involved at all. The recitation becomes a sequence of activations of the "ideo" parts of the ideo-motoric[16] constructs involved in the articulation of voiced vowels. This is the ultimate level of recitation. During it, the separation between successive parts becomes so indistinct that the sequence becomes like a cloud of vague ideas that collapses into voidness at the last part — *aḥ*.

[16] "Ideo-motoric" means connecting mental images with the activation of actions. When an auditory image of a word arises in the consciousness, it has a capacity to evoke an articulation of that word, given the absence of strong inhibitions (like the resolve to be silent, etc.) to do it. This type of connection can be observed when one follows a recitation by another, repeating every word that is said.

Each level of recitation should be repeated several times before going to the next level.

What happens as the result of this gross–subtle–ultimate order is a temporary lessening of the influence of cognitive structures responsible for the automatic introduction of differentiations into cognitive processes, on those very processes. The result of this lessening can produce a transition into the state of *bhairava.*

How to pronounce the sounds:

a is English vowel in *sun*;
ā is English vowel in *far*;
i is English vowel in *fill*;
ī is English vowel in *feel*;
u is English vowel in *put*;
ū is English vowel in *rude*;
e is English vowel in *prey*, not including the final *y*;
ai is English vowel in *aisle*;
o is the first English vowel in *opal*;
au is the English vowel in *out*;

aṃ is like the English *sung* without the *s*; the final sound *ṃ* is a nasal sound that is like the humming vibration when air goes out through the nasal cavity while the mouth is slightly open;

aḥ has no direct equivalent in English. To pronounce it, start pronouncing *us* but relax the tongue before it touches the place where *s* would have been uttered. The movement of the tongue downwards results in air moving into the mouth, as if one is starting to inhale with an open mouth. It sounds like *a*, but with a slight echo after the vowel. This slight echo sound *ḥ* is called *visarga*, and its quality depends on the vowel before it — it resembles the echo of that vowel.

तयापूर्याशु मूर्धान्तं भङ्क्त्वा भ्रूक्षेपसेतुना ।
निर्विकल्पं मनः कृत्वा सर्वोर्ध्वे सर्वगोद्गमः ॥ ३१॥

tayāpūryāśu mūrdhāntaṃ bhaṅktvā bhrūkṣepasetunā |
nirvikalpaṃ manaḥ kṛtvā sarvordhve sarvagodgamaḥ || 31||

When *śakti* is overflowing, using her directly to make a breach in the crown of the head and having *manas* thrown into *sahasrāra-cakra*[17] and de-dichotomized by means of concentration on the spot between the brows, [one will experience] the arising of the All-pervading. Dh. 8

The expression "a breach in the crown of the head" should not be taken literally — it is just a metaphoric description of sensations that occur.

When *śakti* is overflowing — for example, when mental excitation is present, or when habitual emotional or muscular responses to speech are impeded by incisive attention, or through a meditation on the place within where sounds contact with the hearing (mentioned in YS.III.41[18]) — then the excitation can be directed by mental gesture to the top of the skull. Visualize it as the flow of energy breaking through the top of the skull into the space above.

Place the center of awareness (the place from where the "inner eye" is looking) on the top of the skull. With eyes closed, direct the eyes to the spot (of about 2–3mm in size) between the brows, as if trying to see clearly something in that spot.

Maintain all three components (the flow of energy through the top of the skull, the position of the physical eyes, and the location of the inner eye) for several minutes.

The transition to the state of *bhairava*, if it happens, occurs on its own.

[17] See Appendix.
[18] *śrotrākāśayoḥ saṃbandhasaṃyamāddivyaṃ śrotram*

शिखिपक्षैश्चित्ररूपैर्मण्डलैः शून्यपञ्चकम् ।
ध्यायतोऽनुत्तरे शून्ये प्रवेशो हृदये भवेत् ॥ ३२॥

śikhipakṣaiścitrarūpairmaṇḍalaiḥ śūnyapañcakam |
dhyāyato'nuttare śūnye praveśo hṛdaye bhavet || 32||

Dh. 9 By contemplating peacock feathers — how the color and forms of the color spots morph into each other and, finally, into black nothing in the very center — and, in a similar fashion, contemplating sounds, smells, tastes and sensations of touch, while placing *manas* into the *anāhata-cakra*,[19] an entry into the unsurpassed void can occur.

By looking at a peacock feather, contemplate how its color rings morph into each other and how in the center there is only a black (that is, colorless) void. The contemplation has to focus on the fluidity of the perceptions of color, their effortless transitions into each other. Then do a similar contemplation for other senses, while keeping the center of awareness in the *anāhata-cakra*.

It is said "that eyes are form'd to serve the inward light,"[20] and so are the other senses.

[19]See Appendix.
[20]Astrofel and Stella, V

ईदृशेन क्रमेणैव यत्र कुत्रापि चिन्तना ।
शून्ये कुड्ये परे पात्रे स्वयं लीना वरप्रदा ॥ ३३॥

īdṛśena krameṇaiva yatra kutrāpi cintanā |
śūnye kuḍye pare pātre svayaṃ līnā varapradā || 33||

Indeed, she[21] who grants wishes, being contemplated through a similar process,[22] using any object whatsoever, be it empty wall or a bowl far away, dissolves by herself. Dh. 10

Any object that facilitates the grasping of transitions from stable sensations to void, in any modality, can be used instead of a peacock feather (see previous verse).

An empty wall, a drinking cup, a bowl are among the favorite objects of contemplation in many ancient texts, for they can be easily found everywhere; the contemplation will be aided by past philosophical discourses on the emptiness inside the cup, on its form being its essence, etc.

[21] *śakti.*
[22] That is, similar to the one described in the previous verse.

कपालान्तर्मनो न्यस्य तिष्ठन्मीलितलोचनः ।
क्रमेण मनसो दार्ढ्याल्लक्षयेल्लक्ष्यमुत्तमम् ॥ ३४॥

kapālāntarmano nyasya tiṣṭhanmīlitalocanaḥ |
krameṇa manaso dārḍhyāllakṣayellakṣyamuttamam || *34* ||

Dh. 11 Having placed *manas* inside the skull, he who stays with eyes closed, by gradually stabilizing *manas*, might at last notice what is to be noticed.

Sit motionless. Direct your focus of attention into the center of the skull, and narrow your scope of attention to the skull. Close your eyes and keep them closed. Close the "inner eye" of the mind as well, keeping the area where the attention is dwelling in mind by means of a mental gesture. If distracting thoughts arise, gently return attention to that place in the center of the skull. With passing of time the distractions become less frequent. Along with this stabilization of mind comes the opportunity to become subliminally aware of an infinitely extending stillness.

Note that even in complete darkness, eyes should be kept closed, because keeping them closed controls the flow of *kūrma* — the *vāyu* that is responsible for blinking of the eyes.

मध्यनाडी मध्यसंस्था बिससूत्राभरूपया ।
ध्यातान्तर्व्योमया देव्या तया देवः प्रकाशते ॥ ३५॥

madhyanāḍī madhyasaṃsthā bisasūtrābharūpayā |
dhyātāntarvyomayā devyā tayā devaḥ prakāśate || 35||

[When] the middle channel (*suṣumnā*), contained entirely in the middle [of the spine], is meditated upon with [an image of] internally vacuous form like a stalk of lotus, [then] by her, *śakti*, *śiva* is illuminated. Dh. 12

This meditation should be done on a proprioceptive[23] image of the spinal cord superimposed with the visual image of the inside of the lotus stalk.

[23] "Proprioception" is a sense that informs of relative position and the state of muscles, joints, and internal organs.

करुद्धदृगस्त्रेण भ्रूभेदाद्द्वाररोधनात् ।
दृष्टे बिन्दौ क्रमाल्लीने तन्मध्ये परमा स्थितिः ॥ ३६ ॥

kararuddhadṛgastreṇa bhrūbhedāddvārarodhanāt |
dṛṣṭe bindau kramāllīne tanmadhye paramā sthitiḥ || 36||

Dh. 13 With the upper and lower eyelids [of one eye] held by fingers so as to prevent [them from winking] and thus from obstructing the aperture of the eye, and keeping the eyebrows from frowning, when a looked upon dot gradually dissolves — in the midst of that, [there is] ultimate stillness.

Keep the eyelids of one eye open, and thus not winking, by using your fingers. The other eye should be closed, and its eyelid should be relaxed. Do not frown. Look at a luminous dot, such as a lonely star in a dark sky. If attention is kept steady on the dot, the dot will start moving, begin to fade, and then disappear. In that, one will experience the ultimate stillness of the mind.

Swami Lakshman Joo gives a different interpretation of this verse: contemplate the spot between eyebrows and, having made the mind one-pointed by this contemplation, close all openings of the head — eyes, ears, nostrils, mouth — using the fingers of both hands. Maintain the contemplation. In a short while, you will experience a drop of light in front of you; when this light subsides and fades completely, you will enter the state of *śiva*.

धामान्तः क्षोभसम्भूतसूक्ष्माग्नितिलकाकृतिम् ।
बिन्दुं शिखान्ते हृदये लयान्ते ध्यायतो लयः ॥ ३७ ॥

dhāmāntaḥ kṣobhasambhūtasūkṣmāgnitilakākṛtim |
binduṃ śikhānte hṛdaye layānte dhyāyato layaḥ || 37||

Of him who mediates upon a place within, where the mind finds refuge during agitation, as being a well formed[24] spot of subtle fire on the forehead [between the eyebrows], there is a dissolution at the end of the dissolution [of the agitation] at the top of the skull and in the *anāhata-cakra.*[25] Dh. 14

When you feel agitation or anxiety that does not resolve itself into some pattern of behavior, observe where, in the inner space of the mind, the mind tries to find refuge from that agitation. Then, mentally move that place of refuge into the place between the eyebrows. Then, in that very space, make the agitation condense into a fire circle the size of an iris of one's eye. Meditate on that circle, being aware of the sensations on the very top of the skull and in the *anāhata-cakra.* When the traces of agitation dissolve into those two places, then the *bhairava* state has a chance to be manifested.

---

[24]Not fuzzy, quite round and concentrated; the flow through two petals of *ājña-cakra,* if not blocked, causes it to dissipate. In this techniques, this flow should be blocked.

[25]See Appendix.

अनाहते पात्रकर्णेऽभग्नशब्दे सरिद्द्रुते ।
शब्दब्रह्मणि निष्णातः परम्ब्रह्म अधिगच्छति ॥ ३८ ॥

anāhate pātrakarṇe'bhagnaśabde sariddrute |
śabdabrahmaṇi niṣṇātaḥ parambrahma adhigacchati || 38||

Dh. 15 He who in the *anāhata-cakra*[26] is absorbed into the continuous emergence/dissolution of sounds, similar to an uninterrupted, as if streaming, indistinctly spoken speech heard when one puts ear into a big jar, approaches the ultimate Brahma.

Put your ear into the opening of a big jar, a vase, or a sea shell. Listen. The sounds are indistinct, continuous, and ever changing. Now listen to these sounds from the within the *anāhata-cakra* and get drowned in them. It is important to keep the attention on the continuous emergence/dissolution of sounds and to avoid having the attention captured by associations that the sounds might evoke.

[26]See Appendix.

प्रणवादिसमुच्चारात्प्लुतान्ते शून्यभावनात् ।
शून्यया परया शक्त्या शून्यतामेति भैरवि ॥ ३९ ॥

praṇavādisamuccārātplutānte śūnyabhāvanāt |
śūnyayā parayā śaktyā śūnyatāmeti bhairavi || *39*||

From the sensation of emptiness, or void, developing towards the end of a protracted vowel[27] during articulation of a *praṇava*[28] by ineffectual *parā-śakti*, one goes towards the voidness [of the state of *bhairava*], O Bhairavi! Dh. 16

During articulation of the syllable, attention should be on the place where the vowel sound originates and resonates.

This is how to pronounce the sounds:

o in *Oṁ* is pronounced like the first English vowel in *opal.* Alternatively, prepare the voice apparatus to pronounce *ū* as is the English vowel in *rude* and, without changing the position of jaws, tongue, lips, etc., sing *ā* as the English vowel in *far.* That's the protracted *o*. The *ṃ*, which follows *o* in *Oṁ*, is a nasal sound, like a humming vibration when air goes out through the nasal cavity while the mouth is slightly open.

ī of *hrīṃ* is pronounced like the English vowel in *feel.* The *h* at the beginning is pronounced as English *h* in *hut.* The following *r* is pronounced as English *r* in *reef.* The *ṃ* which follows *ī* in *hrīṃ* is a nasal sound that is like the humming vibration when air goes out through the nasal cavity while the mouth is slightly open.

ī of *śrīṃ* is pronounced like the English vowel in *feel.* The *ś* in the beginning is pronounced as the English *s* in *sure.* The following *r* is pronounced as the English *r* in *reef.* The *ṃ* which follows *ī* in *śrīṃ* is a nasal sound that is like a humming vibration when air goes out through the nasal cavity while the mouth is slightly open.

au in *sauḥ* is pronounced like the English vowel in *out*, starting

[27]The vowel is either *o* of *Oṁ*, *ī* of *hrīṃ*, *ī* of *śrīṃ*, or *au* of *sauḥ*.
[28]One of the four mantras *Oṁ*, *hrīṃ*, *śrīṃ*, or *sauḥ*.

with the English vowel in *far* and sliding into the English vowel in *rude.* The final *visarga ḥ* is pronounced as if finishing *ū* with *s* (like the first sound in *sun*), but relaxing the tongue before it touches the place where *s* would have been uttered. The movement of the tongue downwards results in air moving into the mouth, as if one is starting to inhale with an open mouth. It sounds like *ū*, but with a slight echo after it.

यस्य कस्यापि वर्णस्य पूर्वान्तावनुभावयेत् ।
शून्यया शून्यभूतोऽसौ शून्याकारः पुमान्भवेत् ॥ ४० ॥

yasya kasyāpi varṇasya pūrvāntāvanubhāvayet |
śūnyayā śūnyabhūto'sau śūnyākāraḥ pumānbhavet || 40||

If one causes both the first and the last sounds of any syllable, along Dh. 17
with its enveloping emptiness,[29] to produce an impression on the mind, [then] that syllable becomes associated with the void, [and he who is] evoking the void [in this way] might become *bhairava.*[30]

During ordinary speech, sounds are more or less sequential and so are their perceptual, auditory, and tactile impressions on the mind. Here, before uttering the first sound, one should concentrate on the emptiness in the auditory, tactile, and proprioceptive channels of perception, while keeping the impression of this emptiness in short-term memory by maintaining attention on it. Then one should utter the first sound, trying to keep the impression of that first sound in the short-term memory, while uttering and perceiving the last sound. Then, while impressions from both sounds, as well as the emptiness preceding the first sound, are still present in the short-term memory, one should concentrate on the ensuing emptiness in the auditory, tactile, and proprioceptive channels of perception, allowing impressions of the sounds to fade away, while maintaining attention on the void.

After several repetitions, the emptiness encompassing the syllable will become associated with it. Then, uttering the syllable will evoke the void.

[29]This emptiness consists of auditory silence and absence of sensations from the voice apparatus.
[30]Lit. masculine

तन्त्र्यादिवाद्यशब्देषु दीर्घेषु क्रमसंस्थितेः ।
अनन्यचेताः प्रत्यन्ते परव्योमवपुर्भवेत् ॥ ४१ ॥

tantryādivādyaśabdeṣu dīrgheṣu kramasaṃsthiteḥ |
ananyacetāḥ pratyante paravyomavapurbhavet || 41 ||

Dh. 18 If one were to give one's undivided thought to the transitions [that is, the fading away of one and arising of the next,] between prolonged sounds of a string instrument, played in a regular sequence, then, towards the end of the sequence, one might enter the state of the ultimate vacuity [that is, the state of *bhairava*].

पिण्डमन्त्रस्य सर्वस्य स्थूलवर्णक्रमेण तु ।
अर्धेन्दुबिन्दुनादान्तः शून्योच्चाराद्भवेच्छिवः ॥ ४२॥

piṇḍamantrasya sarvasya sthūlavarṇakrameṇa tu |
ardhendubindunādāntaḥ śūnyoccārādbhavecchivaḥ || 42||

[When] by the succession of articulated phonemes of any mantra that ends in *anusvāra* and consists mostly of consonants, [one is at] the verge of the silence at the end of the final stage[31] of the *anusvāra*, then, from the "articulation" of the absence of any phoneme, one can become *śiva*. Dh. 19

Anusvāra is the nasal sound *m* uttered with the nasal passages only, while lips are slightly open. The vibration of this sound spreads the *ājña-cakra*[32] all the way down to *maṇipūra-cakra.*[33] Since the *mantra* used in this practice has mostly consonants, the articulation of it is silent and is, in essence, just a sequence of tension/relaxation that corresponds to the consonants being articulated. The build up of energy that is not released, because of the absence of vowels, is followed by the dissolution of this concentrated energy at the very end of the *anusvāra.* This dissolution can uncover the state of *śiva.*

An example of such a *mantra*, given by J.Singh, is a *navātma:*
h-r-kṣ-m-l-v-y-ṇ-ūṃ

The sound *kṣ* is pronounced as English *ct* in *fiction*; *ṇ* as *n* in *none.* For other sounds, see the verse 39.

---

[31] Called *candrabindu.*
[32] The place between the brows. See Appendix.
[33] Approximately, the solar plexus. See Appendix.

निजदेहे सर्वदिक्कं युगपद्भावयेद्वियत् ।
निर्विकल्पमनास्तस्य वियत्सर्वं प्रवर्तते ॥ ४३ ॥

nijadehe sarvadikkaṃ yugapadbhāvayedviyat |
nirvikalpamanāstasya viyatsarvaṃ pravartate || 43||

Dh. 20 If one were to form in the mind an image of all space directions simultaneously, as they are given in the sensations of the body, [and to spread the attention evenly to all six of them — up, down, right, left, front, and back,] then, in consequence of the mind becoming devoid of polarizations,[34] everything "his" would be vanishing.

Sit in a comfortable posture, spine straight, head well balanced, so the neck is not strained. With eyes closed, feel the space around you, in particular, the well defined directions up, down, front, back, left, and right, as if some thin threads are slightly pulling from each of those directions. Let the impressions of all six directions be present at once in the mind, with equal attention on each of them. After this distribution of attention is maintained for a few minutes, the mind might slip into a state in which no pair of opposite ideas (like good–evil, pleasant–painful, noble–lowly) frames perception or cognition. Then, all personal constructs projecting prominently onto the axis "mine–not-mine" recede into the shadows, and the mind dissolves into "the vast expanse of consciousness" (in J.Singh's words).

This technique is based on the observation that personal constructs that project prominently onto the axis "mine–not-mine" tend to project onto body postures. Preventing this habitual projection results in a *śakti* that illuminates *śiva.*

[34] *Vikalpa*-s.

Verses 44, 45, 46 refer to emptiness, or void, in the subtle body.

पृष्ठशून्यं मूलशून्यं युगपद्भावयेच्च यः ।
शरीरनिरपेक्षिण्या शक्त्या शून्यमना भवेत् ॥ ४४ ॥

pṛṣṭhaśūnyaṃ mūlaśūnyaṃ yugapadbhāvayecca yaḥ |
śarīranirapekṣiṇyā śaktyā śūnyamanā bhavet || 44 ||

He who is able to cause the void in the top [of the skull] and the void in the root to appear simultaneously, through the *śakti* that becomes independent of the supporting frame, might become the one whose mental disposition is the voidness. Dh. 21

Here, "the top of the skull" means *sahasrāra-cakra*;[35] "the root" means *mūladhāra-cakra*; and "the supporting frame" means the subtle body.

The void is "caused to appear" in any particular spot by the following technique: Concentrate on that spot. Whatever sensation appears there, let it arise and fade away, without allowing it to capture attention by a chain of associations. If the attention floats away, return it gently onto the same spot. Within a few minutes, the void might appear. If not, then become aware of a persistent, cloud-like sensation in that spot; analyze its origin, and attempt to destabilize it.

In this verse, one should attempt to make the void appear in both the *sahasrāra-cakra* and the *mūladhāra-cakra*. Initially, make the void appear in one, then the other; then divide the attention equally between the two, but avoid the explicit intention of doing so. When both voids manifest, the sensory image of the subtle body might collapse. If this happens, do not try to resurrect it — just let the void be — and become *Śiva*-like.

[35] See Appendix.

पृष्ठशून्यं मूलशून्यं हृच्छून्यं भावयेत्स्थिरम् ।
युगपन्निर्विकल्पत्वान्निर्विकल्पोदयस्ततः ॥ ४५॥

pṛṣṭhaśūnyaṃ mūlaśūnyaṃ hṛcchūnyaṃ bhāvayetsthiram |
yugapannirvikalpatvānnirvikalpodayastataḥ || *45*||

Dh. 22 If one were to cause the void in the very top of the head, the void in the *mūladhāra-cakra,*[36] and the void in the *anāhata-cakra* to appear in a stable fashion, then, at that moment, from the absence of polarization [in the subtle body], would arises the absence of polarizations [in the mind].

How to cause the void to appear in a particular spot is explained in the previous verse. "Polarization" is explained in the chapter "Concepts" in the *vikalpa* entry.

In this verse, the void should be allowed to pervade *sahasrāra-cakra*, *mūladhāra-cakra*, and *anāhata-cakra.*[37] When this happens in all three of them, the subtle body becomes devoid of connections with the emotional centers of the mind, which, in its turn, becomes without a frame of support and disperses like smoke into the blue sky.

[36] See Appendix.
[37] See Appendix.

तनूदेशे शून्यतैव क्षणमात्रं विभावयेत् ।
निर्विकल्पं निर्विकल्पो निर्विकल्पस्वरूपभाक् ॥ ४६॥

tanūdeśe śūnyataiva kṣaṇamātraṃ vibhāvayet |
nirvikalpaṃ nirvikalpo nirvikalpasvarūpabhāk || 46||

If one were to transform, even for a moment, the [sensation of] emptiness in some part of the [physical] body into distinct absence of polarizations (*vikalpa*-s), [then that state of the] absence of *vikalpa*-s would exhibit [one's own] true nature, devoid of *vikalpa*-s. Dh. 23

This technique is based on the observation that polarizations (*vikalpa*) tend to project onto the subtle body as a sense of a mist or a cloud of something in various parts of the body. If somewhere there is emptiness, for whatever reason, then the polarizations temporarily lose support and one can drift into the state where no active polarizations are present.

If a sensation of emptiness is detected in any part of the body, just get absorbed into it. The only additional action one needs to take is to dissolve any intent to get alternative support for those polarizations that might appear, and to absorb one's attention into the feeling of emptiness.

सर्वं देहगतं द्रव्यं वियद्व्याप्तं मृगेक्षणे ।
विभावयेत्ततस्तस्य भावना सा स्थिरा भवेत् ॥ ४७॥

sarvaṃ dehagataṃ dravyaṃ viyadvyāptaṃ mṛgekṣaṇe |
vibhāvayettatastasya bhāvanā sā sthirā bhavet || 47||

Dh. 24 If one were to visualize each material substance in the body (bones, flesh, blood, marrow, etc.) to be thoroughly pervaded by the ether (as smoke is pervaded by the air), O Gazelle-eyed one, then his realization [of his own true nature, devoid of *vikalpa*-s,] would become lasting.

The "ether" here denotes "that which converts sounds into speech." Try to contemplate how a sound is converted into speech in inner space. What is the connection between hearing sound and hearing speech, as it is represented in the space of introspection? Contemplate the transition of sounds to speech, as mediated by some substance — "ether." Then, imagine vividly that this ether pervades all material substances of the body — bones, flesh, blood, marrow, brain tissue, etc. — and, thus, the transition sound–speech is occurring everywhere in the body, with no boundaries or particular localization. Maintaining this conception throughout the hustle and bustle of the day would result in subtle, steady awareness of the state of *bhairava.*

देहान्तरे त्वग्विभागं भित्तिभूतं विचिन्तयेत् ।
नकिंचिदन्तरे तस्य ध्यायन्नध्येयभाग्भवेत् ॥ ४८ ॥

dehāntare tvagvibhāgaṃ bhittibhūtaṃ vicintayet |
nakiṃcidantare tasya dhyāyannadhyeyabhāgbhavet || 48||

If one were to observe, as if from inside the body, one's own skin as a wall-like barrier, [then,] meditating on the emptiness inside that barrier, one would be enjoying that which cannot be imagined. Dh. 25

हृद्याकाशे निलीनाक्षः पद्मसम्पुटमध्यगः ।
अनन्यचेताः सुभगे परं सौभाग्यमाप्नुयात् ॥ ४९ ॥

hṛdyākāśe nilīnākṣaḥ padmasampuṭamadhyagaḥ |
ananyacetāḥ subhage paraṃ saubhāgyamāpnuyāt || 49||

Dh. 26 There is an axis hidden in the region of the *anāhata-cakra*[38] that goes through the middle of the hemisphere of the lotus flower [of the *cakra*]. He who minds nothing else but this [image],O fortunate one, might attain the ultimate fortune [of experiencing the state of *bhairava*].

An image of the *anāhata-cakra* is painted by sensations of *prāṇa* and *apāna* flowing through it, not by visual images of petals/lotus. Petals of a *cakra* are sensations of directional flows to/from the central spot of the *cakra*, which is about a thumb-width in diameter.

The axis is the flow of *prāṇa* and *apāna* from *maṇipūra* to the *viśuddha-cakra*.

Ordinarily, this axis passes behind the *anāhata-cakra*. The essence of this technique is in altering the relative location of these two images, so that the axis is passing through the middle of the *anāhata-cakra*.

If one concentrates on nothing else but this combined image, it causes one to be "thrown towards the center" and to become as if immersed into an aura of subtle vibration.

Then, if that subtle vibration is prevented from giving rise to a train of thought or to mental gestures, the state of *bhairava* becomes manifest.

---

[38]See Appendix.

सर्वतः स्वशरीरस्य द्वादशान्ते मनोलयात् ।
दृढबुद्धेर्दृढीभूतं तत्त्वलक्ष्यं प्रवर्तते ॥ ५० ॥

sarvataḥ svaśarīrasya dvādaśānte manolayāt |
dṛḍhabuddherdṛḍhībhūtaṃ tattvalakṣyaṃ pravartate || 50||

If one were to dissolve *manas* in the area that is twelve thumb-widths from one's own body in every direction, then, from the steady awareness [in such a state], the indication of of *śiva-tattva*[39] would grow stronger. Dh. 27

Sit comfortably. Close your eyes and scan the skin of your body. Now imagine a surface outside of the body that is about twelve thumb-widths outside of the skin (measure with a ruler this distance before the exercise and see where this distance is from various parts of the body, to get the correct idea). Next, place the spot from where your attention originates somewhere on that surface. As a result, the mind's eye will be observing the body and other sensory stimuli as if from that surface. Let the location of the mind's eye on that surface change so that, instead of a spot, the origin of attention becomes the whole surface. Maintain steady awareness of all stimuli that appear, avoiding any train of thought.

[39]For *śiva-tattva* cannot be perceived directly, but only through expression of *śakti*.

यथा तथा यत्र तत्र द्वादशान्ते मनः क्षिपेत् ॥
प्रतिक्षणं क्षीणवृत्तेर्वैलक्षण्यं दिनैर्भवेत् ॥ ५१ ॥

yathā tathā yatra tatra dvādaśānte manaḥ kṣipet ||
pratikṣaṇaṃ kṣīṇavṛttervailakṣaṇyaṃ dinairbhavet || *51* ||

Dh. 28 If one were to continually cast *manas* into *dvādaśānta*, however and in whatever circumstances, then, from the waning of the evoked cognitive dynamic,[40] contrast [between the background of *śiva-tattva* and foreground of sensory impressions] would increase daily.

Here *dvādaśānta* means "the spot twelve thumb-widths above the top of the skull." In this technique, the spot from where the attention originates is consciously moved into *dvādaśānta* continually, throughout the day. As a result, the mind's eye will be observing the body from outside and above the head.

[40]Denoted in Yoga Sutra with term *vṛtti*.

कालाग्निना कालपदादुत्थितेन स्वकम् पुरम् ।
प्लुष्टं विचिन्तयेदन्ते शान्ताभासस्तदा भवेत् ॥ ५२॥

kālāgninā kālapadādutthitena svakam puram |
pluṣṭaṃ vicintayedante śāntābhāsastadā bhavet || 52||

If one were to observe the fortress of one's own body to be [as if] burned by [what feels like] fire arising from the big toe of the right leg, then, at the end of the destruction, the mind would be a reflection of the tranquility [that is on the verge of the state of *bhairava*]. Dh. 29

The sensation described here is very real. It feels as if flames, burning upon touch, arise from the big toe of the right leg and spread upwards in the body, leaving behind emptiness. The onset of this sensation might result from various conditions; for example, in the state of recoil from contact, even mental contact, with personally significant people. The anguish and dejection that might accompany such a state urges one to act and escape this state of mind. If, instead, one just observes the arising and development of the sensation of being burned, while maintaining full awareness, without inhibiting the upper *cakra*-s[41] and seeking no refuge, then deep tranquility sets in.

This fire is called the "fire of the total destruction," or *kāla-agni*.

Osho recommends observing the burning of dead bodies on burning grounds as part of this technique.

[41] See Appendix.

एवमेव जगत्सर्वं दग्धं ध्यात्वा विकल्पतः ।
अनन्यचेतसः पुंसः पुम्भावः परमो भवेत् ॥ ५३॥

evameva jagatsarvaṃ dagdhaṃ dhyātvā vikalpataḥ |
ananyacetasaḥ puṃsaḥ pumbhāvaḥ paramo bhavet || 53||

Dh. 30 Verily, if one were to meditate unhesitatingly upon the entire world of living beings being consumed by fire, then the *bhairava* aspect would become distinctly manifested.

स्वदेहे जगतो वापि सूक्ष्मसूक्ष्मतराणि च ।
तत्त्वानि यानि निलयं ध्यात्वान्ते व्यज्यते परा ॥ ५४॥

svadehe jagato vāpi sūkṣmasūkṣmatarāṇi ca |
tattvāni yāni nilayaṃ dhyātvānte vyajyate parā || 54||

Having imagined the subtle and beyond-subtle *tattva*-s of every living creature to repose in one's own body, one makes the ultimate *śakti*, as if etched [into the conscious awareness as the state of *bhairava*]. Dh. 31

Here is a detailed variant of this practice:

1. Bring to mind your own body as fully as possible — as a visual image, as sensations on the skin, as smells, as proprioceptive signals, etc.

2. For each and every living creature that comes to mind, imagine the relish of preferences/aversions, that is an active pattern structuring the mental processes of that creature, to repose inside your own body (as brought to mind in step 1).

3. For each and every living creature that comes to mind, imagine the inhibition, that is an active pattern structuring mental processes of that creature, to repose inside your own body (as brought to mind in step 1).

4. For each and every living creature that comes to mind, imagine the formation of meanings (especially of meanings, relevant to survival), that are an active pattern structuring mental processes of that creature, to repose inside your own body (as brought to mind in step 1).

5. For each and every living creature that comes to mind, imagine the sense of necessity, that is an active pattern structuring mental processes of that creature, to repose inside your own body (as brought to mind in step 1).

6. For each and every living creature that comes to mind, imagine its set points in time or set durations, that are active patterns structuring mental processes of that creature, to repose inside your own body (as brought to mind in step 1).

Maintain attention on all of the active patterns from 2–6 as reposing in your own body (as brought to mind in step 1), and observe how everything living becomes part of you.

पीनां च दुर्बलां शक्तिं ध्यात्वा द्वादशगोचरे ।
प्रविश्य हृदये ध्यायन्मुक्तः स्वातन्त्र्यमाप्नुयात् ॥ ५५॥

pīnāṃ ca durbalāṃ śaktiṃ dhyātvā dvādaśagocare |
praviśya hṛdaye dhyāyan muktaḥ svātantryamāpnuyāt || 55||

If, having meditated on the energy [of breathing] as being weak and compacted inside the area within twelve thumb-widths from the body, one were to meditate on this energy as permeating the *anāhata-cakra*[42] [and falls asleep while doing that], then, becoming free [from the waking state and the dreaming state], one might attain [uncommitted] self-will. Dh. 32

In this verse, to meditate on the energy of breathing is to meditate on the subtle tension that causes one to breath in and on the subtle tension that causes one to breath out.

Śiva Svarodaya states that the mental representation of the energy of breathing has an extension that varies with conditions. At rest, the extension is about twelve thumb-widths from the nostrils;[43] during strenuous physical activity it may be extend to as much as 65 widths.[44] Attaining various extraordinary abilities is connected with reducing this distance to less then twelve widths. The more it is reduced, the more the faculties related to advancement in yoga develop. Shortening the extension is tied to the distance at which the air around the nose is disturbed by breathing, so in order to progress in this, one needs to practice *prāṇāyāma.*

Self-will is inherent in the nature of consciousness, so self-will cannot be attained *per se.* In the course of constructing the mind, self-will becomes committed to various configurations of *tattva*-s, so that the energy of the will is dissipated into pre-established patterns of thinking, acting, and feeling. Some of this energy can be made uncommitted, as a result of specially designed practices like this one.

What does it mean "to become free from the waking state and the dreaming state"?

---

[42] See Appendix.
[43] *prāṇasya tu gatirdevi svabhāvadvādaśāṅgula* ShSv.223.a.
[44] ShSv.222.

Of the various states and modes that consciousness functions in, understanding the phases of wakefulness, dreaming, deep sleep, and "the fourth" are of particular importance to practices of this tantra.

The short exposition below follows Swami Rama's book [Ram82], which is a commentary to the *Māṇḍukya* Upanishad.

The first mode of consciousness is the waking state, *vaiśvānara*. It tunes into the gross external [stimuli].[45] The content of consciousness is filtered by the Ego and is characterized by subject-object polarization.

The second mode of consciousness is the dreaming state, *taijasa*. It tunes into the internal plane (fantasies, dreams, projections of desires) and partakes of isolation (from the gross and the external).[46] The subject-object duality is still present, but it is somewhat less rigid than in the waking state.

The third mode of consciousness is the abiding in deep sleep. When one is insensible [to external stimuli], desiring nothing, and dreaming nothing, that state is deep sleep.[47]

This third mode, called *prājña*, has no subject-object duality. It is an ocean of pure cognitions, in which one is saturated with bliss and experiencing it. It has only one aspect — attentiveness.[48] In this mode, the unconscious is in the scope of awareness, and the fog of perceptual experiences and memories is not present to interfere with knowing it.

These three modes might be called perceptual, imaginative, and conceptual states, respectively.

Breaking barriers between these states is important for reversing the contractions of *citi* and, thus, for dissolving their isolation and autonomy. In order to break these barriers, one should transcend into another mode, or state of consciousness, called "the fourth."

"The fourth" is characterized as follows:

> It is preeminent among all other states;
> it experiences and knows every other state;

---

[45] *jāgaritasthāno bahiḥprajñaḥ saptāṅga ekonaviṃśatimukhaḥ sthūlabhugvaiśvānaraḥ prathamaḥ pādaḥ* ManUp.3.

[46] *svapnasthāno'ntaprajñaḥ saptāṅga ekaviṃśatimukhaḥ praviviktabhuktaijaso dvitīyaḥ pādaḥ* ManUp.4.

[47] *yatra supto na kañcana kāmaṃ kāmayate na kañcana svapnaṃ paśyati tatsuṣuptam* ManUp.5.a.

[48] *suṣuptasthāna ekībhūtaḥ prajñānaghana evānandamayo hyānandabhuk cetomukhaḥ prājñastṛtīyaḥ pādaḥ* ManUp.5.b.

it regulates the inner feelings;
it is the source of every other state;
in it is the origination and dissolution
of all mental phenomena.[49]

One thinks of it as
neither tuning into the internal plane,
nor tuning into the external plane,
nor tuning into both planes at once;
as neither pure awareness,
nor attention,
nor non-attention;
as unobserved, not experienced during
the ordinary course of life (unlike the three other states),
ungraspable by intuition,
having no prior signs (or symptoms).[50]

It is unimaginable, undefinable by means of verbal expression; it consists primarily of self-supporting *buddhi*; it is soothing the proliferation of illusions caused by the employment of language; it is free from passions, happy, having no dualities. It is the real Self that is to be discerned in its pure form.[51]

Here is a practice that aims at breaking barriers between perceptual, imaginative, and conceptual states.

It is outlined in the *sūtra*-s 8–12 of the *Māṇḍūkya* Upanishad. One has to realize that the waking state, *vaiśvānara*, is emphasized by concentration on *ājña-cakra*[52] and by articulation of the sound *a*; that the dreaming state, *taijasa*, is emphasized by concentration on *viśuddha-cakra* and by articulation of the sound *u*; that the deep sleep state, *prājña*, is emphasized by concentration on *anāhata-cakra* and by articulation of the sound *ṃ*. Then, by articulation of *a-u-ṃ*, with the corresponding shift of concentrated attention to *ājña-cakra* – *viśuddha-cakra* – *anāhata-cakra* for extended periods of time, the articulation of sounds is merged into *Oṁ*, and the consciousness is pulled towards"the fourth." The shift to *prājña*

[49] *eṣa sarveśvara eṣasarvajña eṣo'ntaryāmyeṣa yoniḥ sarvasya prabhavāpyayau hi bhūtānām* ManUp.6

[50] *nāntaḥprajñaṃ na bahiṣprajñaṃ nobhayataḥprajñaṃ na prajñānaghanaṃ na prajñaṃ nāprajñamadṛṣṭamavyavahāryamagrāhyamalakśaṇaṃ* ManUp.7.a

[51] *acintyamavyapadeśyamekātmapratyayasāraṃ prapañcopaśamaṃ śāntaṃ śivamadvaitaṃ caturthaṃ manyante sa ātmā sa vijñeyaḥ* ManUp.7.b

[52] See Appendix.

can be learned. A practice to do this is called *yoga-nidrā*, or "yogic sleep." Details can be found in [Ram96].

Getting back to the practice of this verse, when the expressions of the waking and dreaming states lose their strength, one slips into deep sleep, which saturates mind with pure bliss. Even after waking up, this saturation provides the support to keep some of the self-will in the uncommitted, liminal state. And this liminality can lead to the state of *bhairava*.

भुवनाध्वादि रूपेण चिन्तयेत्क्रमशोऽखिलम् ।
स्थूलसूक्ष्मपरस्थित्या यावदन्ते मनोलयः ॥ ५६ ॥

bhuvanādhvādi rūpeṇa cintayetkramaśo'khilam |
sthūlasūkṣmaparasthityā yāvadante manolayaḥ || *56* ||

One might contemplate the objective track [of manifestation] in its entirety, using a material object [like a jar, etc.], while maintaining gross-subtle-ultimate [order], until finally — dissolution of *manas* [occurs]. Dh. 33

The objective track of manifestation, called *bhuvanā-adhvan*, consists of three stages: *bhuvanā*-stage, *tattva*-stage, and *kalā*-stage.

The *bhuvanā*-stage is when whole objects are manifested; this is gross manifestation. The *tattva*-stage is when features of objects are manifested, but features are not objects themselves; this is subtle manifestation. The *kalā*-stage is when not even features are present, but only variations of the perceptual field are manifest; this is the ultimate manifestation.

Imagine moving closer and closer to a painting made with distinct strokes, without losing sight of any part of the painting. Initially the whole image of the painting is seen; then, as one gets too closer, only parts are seen, like curves, lines, color blots, etc. When one gets even closer, only variations of the visual field are seen and none of the distinct features of the painting. That's how the objective track of manifestation should be contemplated, while keeping attention on a particular physical object.

This process of disintegration of a visual picture, from gross to subtle and from subtle to ultimate, happens naturally during *bhairavī-mudrā* that is described thus in the commentary to *sūtra* 18 of *Pratyabhijñāhṛdayam* thus: "Attention is concentrated on an internal object, but sense organs are fully open to external objects, while keeping open eyes from winking or wandering."[53]

---

[53] *antarlakṣyo bahirdṛṣṭiḥ nimeṣonmeṣavarjitaḥ*

अस्य सर्वस्य विश्वस्य पर्यन्तेषु समन्ततः ।
अध्वप्रक्रियया तत्त्वं शैवं ध्यत्वा महोदयः ॥ ५७॥

asya sarvasya viśvasya paryanteṣu samantataḥ |
adhvaprakriyayā tattvaṃ śaivaṃ dhyatvā mahodayaḥ || 57||

Dh. 34 If one were to meditate upon the *śiva-tattva*, by disintegrating every object and every substance of the manifested world, using the procedure of the *adhvan*-analysis explained in the previous verse, then [one might experience] the arising of the ultimate.

विश्वमेतन्महादेवि शून्यभूतं विचिन्तयेत् ।
तत्रैव च मनोलीनं ततस्तल्लयभाजनम् ॥ ५८ ॥

viśvametanmahādevi śūnyabhūtaṃ vicintayet |
tatraiva ca manolīnaṃ tatastallayabhājanam || *58* ||

If, O *Mahādevī*, one were to imagine this Universe as being essen- Dh. 35
tially empty and to imagine the dissolution of mind in that very emptiness, then one would partake of this dissolution [and enter the state of *bhairava*].

To "imagine this Universe as being essentially empty" can be done by mentally dissolving patterns of earth, water, air, and fire (see entry *mahābhūta*-s in the "Concepts" chapter). This dissolving can be done, for example, by contemplating transitions in the sequence of putting ghee into a sacrificial fire: it is hard at first, then it turns liquid, then the liquid becomes flames, then the flames dissipate and vanish to become air, then the air is full of smells, and finally smells dissipates into the void.

Likewise, mind is dissolved into the void upon the dissolution of the patterns — since it is supported by reflecting and by imposing these patterns.

घटादिभाजने दृष्टिं भित्तीस्त्यक्त्वा विनिक्षिपेत् ।
तल्लयं तत्क्षणाद्गत्वा तल्लयात्तन्मयोभवेत् ॥ ५९ ॥

ghaṭādibhājane dṛṣṭiṃ bhittīstyaktvā vinikṣipet |
tallayaṃ tatkṣaṇādgatvā tallayāttanmayobhavet || *59* ||

Dh. 36 If one were to fix the gaze upon a jar, etc., (that is, a material object with well defined boundaries), having abandoned the boundaries [by relaxing attention bias on them and by letting go of patterns that support the perception of boundaries], and having immediately entered [with one's attention] the dissolution of that [image of the object] as it occurs, [then] one might become identical with the void resulting from that dissolution.

निर्वृक्षगिरिभित्त्यादिदेशे दृष्टिं विनिक्षिपेत् ।
विलीने मानसे भावे वृत्तिक्षिणः प्रजायते ॥ ६० ॥

nirvṛkṣagiribhittyādideśe dṛṣṭiṃ vinikṣipet |
vilīne mānase bhāve vṛttikṣiṇaḥ prajāyate || 60||

If one were to gaze at a spot on a treeless mountain, clear wall, etc., then, during the dissolution [in consequence of gazing] of mental dispositions, [for example, striving for something or avoiding or resisting something,] the diminution of the evoked cognitive dynamic[54] would be conceived. Dh. 37

[54]Denoted in Yoga Sutra with term *vṛtti*.

उभयोर्भावयोर्ज्ञाने ध्यात्वा मध्यं समाश्रयेत् ।
युगपच्च द्वयं त्यक्त्वा मध्ये तत्त्वं प्रकाशते ॥ ६१॥

ubhayorbhāvayorjñāne dhyātvā madhyaṃ samāśrayet |
yugapacca dvayaṃ tyaktvā madhye tattvaṃ prakāśate || 61||

Dh. 38 If, having meditated on experiencing both [kinds of] sentiments,[55] one were to relax into an intermediate disposition; and, having simultaneously let go of both [sentiments by having stopped supporting attention on them]; [then,] in [that] intermediate [state of mind], the [*śiva-*]*tattva* becomes manifest.

Recollect in vivid personal detail (images, sounds, smells, touch, taste, feelings) two opposite experiences; for example, an experience of being praised by a beautiful woman and an experience of being reproached by a beautiful woman. Bring to mind both recollections and the acute feelings evoked; distribute attention equally between them. Let go of both (for example, with an "I can do without it" mental gesture) and observe both from an intermediate attitude (position or mindset) with full awareness. The vastness of the inner equanimity might just flash forth.

[55] Striving for something and avoiding or resisting the opposite.

भावे त्यक्ते निरुद्धा चिन्नैव भावान्तरं व्रजेत् ।
तदा तन्मध्यभावेन विकसत्यति भावना ॥ ६२ ॥

bhāve tyakte niruddhā cinnaiva bhāvāntaraṃ vrajet |
tadā tanmadhyabhāvena vikasatyati bhāvanā || 62 ||

If, having abandoned a sentiment, the thought is constrained so Dh. 39
that it does not wander towards another sentiment, then, through [the resulting] intermediate disposition, the realization [of the state of *bhairava*] is brought to light.

When you feel strongly about pursuing something, or avoiding something, or possessing/getting rid of something, or being proud/ashamed of something, etc., let that feeling go. Take care not to fall into an opposite or related sentiment. If you can avoid adopting another sentiment, then the emptiness left from the original strong feeling deconstructs the mental fabrications that were based on that feeling. The scaffolds of perception and cognition propped up by the feeling crumble, and one experiences again the blooming of the primeval consciousness.

सर्वं देहं चिन्मयं हि जगद्वा परिभावयेत् ।
युगपन्निर्विकल्पेन मनसा परमोदयः ॥ ६३॥

sarvaṃ dehaṃ cinmayaṃ hi jagadvā paribhāvayet |
yugapannirvikalpena manasā paramodayaḥ || 63||

Dh. 40 If one were to mentally conceive the entire body or, alternatively, this world of sentient beings as consisting of pure attention or of thought, then, simultaneously with the mind [becoming] free from *vikalpa*-s (polarizations), [there would be] the arising of the ultimate.

In order to correctly conceive the entire body as nothing but pure thought, one has to have

1. experiences of awareness of various parts of the body, as well as the experience of conscious withdrawal of such awareness;

2. experiences of changing one's body posture through one's aspirations and intentions;

3. experiences of changing sensations of pain or pleasure into neutral sensations by means of thought; and experiences of controlling the various states of the body with the mind.

Then, having painted the image of the body with particular thoughts that give rise to various states and conditions in the body, one would conceive the entire body as nothing but pure thought.

Similarly, the whole world of sentient beings might be conceived as nothing but pure thought, if one were to contemplate the above experiences as present in all sentient beings.

वायुद्वयस्य संघट्टादन्तर्वा बहिरन्ततः ।
योगी समत्वविज्ञानसमुद्गमनभाजनम् ॥ ६४ ॥

vāyudvayasya saṃghaṭṭādantarvā bahirantataḥ |
yogī samatvavijñānasamudgamanabhājanam || 64||

From recurring collisions of overlapping flows of *prāṇa* and *apāna*, Dh. 41
either when breathing in wanes and breathing out waxes or when breathing out wanes and breathing in waxes, the yogi experiences simultaneous arising of the discernment and equanimity.

To evoke the collision of overlapping flows of *prāṇa* and *apāna*, one needs the ability to control these two flows by means of mental gestures.

When unobstructed breathing in starts coming to an end, evoke the flow of *apāna* without interrupting the breathing in. Two flows will be present and the collision will occur. At some point, the expression of *prāṇa* will be of approximately the same intensity as the expression of *apāna*. This equilibrium is what induces the desired state of equanimity.

Similarly, the collision happens in the case when breathing out starts coming to an end. After several such cycles of breathing, the state of *bhairava* has a chance to become manifest.

Compare this technique with Dh.2 (verse 25).

सर्वं जगत् स्वदेहं वा स्वानन्दभरितं स्मरेत् ।
युगपत्स्वामृतेनैव परानन्दमयो भवेत् ॥ ६५ ॥

sarvaṃ jagatsvadehaṃ vā svānandabharitaṃ smaret |
yugapatsvāmṛtenaiva parānandamayo bhavet || 65 ||

Dh. 42 If one were to imagine all sentient beings or, alternatively, one's own body to be nourished to satiation by the inner bliss, then, simultaneously with the flow of one's own ambrosia,[56] one might become as if made of the ultimate bliss.

Having experienced an overflow of bliss is a prerequisite for this practice. When imagining one's own body, one should concentrate in sequence on all *cakra*-s,[57] all joints, all areas of heightened sensitivity, like finger tips, lips, etc., and imagine recollected feelings of overflowing bliss pervading each area of concentration.

[56] Likely, it is beta-endorphin originating in the pituitary gland.
[57] See Appendix.

कुहनेन प्रयोगेण सद्य एव मृगेक्षणे ।
समुदेति महानन्दो येन तत्त्वं प्रकाशते ॥ ६६ ॥

kuhanena prayogeṇa sadya eva mṛgekṣaṇe |
samudeti mahānando yena tattvaṃ prakāśate || 66||

Along with [attentively observing] an astonishing presentation of magic (e.g., card tricks seen close up), O Gazelle-eyed, there always arises a great joy by which [that] *tattva* becomes manifest. Dh. 43

Allow your attention to be totally immersed into the amazement arising from watching magic tricks or from new inventions of science and technology — whatever causes the sense of wonder. Let your whole mind be filled with that sense, leaving criticisms and doubts for later. As an after-effect of the sense of deep wonder, the state of *bhairava* is manifested.

सर्वस्रोतोनिबन्धेन प्राणशक्त्योर्ध्वया शनैः ।
पिपीलस्पर्शवेलायां प्रथते परमं सुखम् ॥ ६७॥

sarvasrotonibandhena prāṇaśaktyordhvayā śanaiḥ |
pipīlasparśavelāyāṃ prathate paramaṃ sukham || 67||

Dh. 44 Through a contraction of all streams [of subtle energies towards organs of perception and organs of action] by the energy of breath (*prāṇa-śakti*) gradually moving upwards [along the spine], an exceptional [feeling of] comfort spreads [through the body] at the moment of a tingling sensation [as if ants are crawling on the skin].

Direct all organs of perception inside by concentrating them on the area around the *svādhiṣṭhāna-cakra.*[58] Look into that area, hear that area, etc. Allow the energy of the breath to go up the spine without constraints or blocks. Drain the senses of energy, as if you have fainted, and be oblivious to sensations. After breathing out, effortlessly refrain from breathing in until the breath returns naturally. Keep breathing this way. If the breathing in is delayed long enough you might feel tingling sensations along the spine and maybe in some other parts of the body. At this moment a deep bliss — that feels more like a warm bath than a glass of champagne —spreads, .

[58]See Appendix.

वह्नेर्विषस्य मध्ये तु चित्तं सुखमयं क्षिपेत् ।
केवलं वायुपूर्णं वा स्मरानन्देन युज्यते ॥ ६८ ॥

vahnerviṣasya madhye tu cittaṃ sukhamayaṃ kṣipet |
kevalaṃ vāyupūrṇaṃ vā smarānandena yujyate || 68||

If one were to cast into the middle [channel] comforting thoughts Dh. 45
of a burning fire and to imagine [the middle channel] to be filled only with *prāṇa*, then one would be united with the recollected afterglow [of sexual love; and in that recollection one would get close to the state of *bhairava*].

When "imagining the middle channel to be filled only with *prāṇa*," place the urge, the tension to breathe in, entirely into the stem of the spine, but do not hold the breath or interfere with it. Let the mind and your whole being be immersed into that afterglow.

शक्तिसंगमसंक्षुब्धशक्त्यावेशावसानिकम् ।
यत्सुखं ब्रह्मतत्त्वस्य तत्सुखं स्वाक्यमुच्यते ॥ ६९ ॥

śaktisaṃgamasaṃkṣubdhaśaktyāveśāvasānikam |
yatsukhaṃ brahmatattvasya tatsukhaṃ svākyamucyate || *69*||

Dh. 46 It is said that the comfort that is unveiled at the end of taking possession of a female consort, to him who is violently shaken by the contact with the consort, is the comfort [inherent in] the infinite plasticity [of one's own Self].

This technique is based on a tantric sexual practice. It consists in having continuous sexual contact with a female consort, while maintaining sexual arousal for thirty minutes or more and relaxing most of the body. Any movement should be at a minimal level, just sufficient for maintaining the arousal. This leads to gradually increasing tension, and at some point the tension will result in waves of shaking that spread through the body. Only if this shaking occurs, then, after the natural release of the tension at the point where it cannot be maintained any longer, one is satiated and is on the verge of the deep calm, full of all possibilities.

लेहनामन्थनाकोटैः स्त्रीसुखस्य भरात्स्मृतेः ।
शक्त्यभावेऽपि देवेशि भवेदानन्दसम्प्लवः ॥ ७० ॥

lehanāmanthanākoṭaiḥ strīsukhasya bharātsmṛteḥ |
śaktyabhāve'pi deveśi bhavedānandasamplavaḥ || 70||

Through intense recollection of the delight from licking, rubbing, or being embraced by a woman, O Devi, one might experience a flood of bliss — even in the absence of a female consort. Dh. 47

The attention should be focused on the recollected sensations, or raw impressions of the delight, that results from the show of affection from a woman. Any caresses that made one feel as if melted with pleasure and that caused one to forget himself can be recollected. This flood of bliss brings one to the verge of experiencing the state of *bhairava.*

आनन्दे महति प्राप्ते दृष्टे वा बान्धवे चिरात् ।
आनन्दमुद्गतं ध्यात्वा तल्लयस्तन्मना भवेत् ॥ ७१॥

ānande mahati prāpte dṛṣṭe vā bāndhave cirāt |
ānandamudgataṃ dhyātvā tallayastanmanā bhavet || 71||

Dh. 48 Having meditated upon the bliss that instantly arises at the moment of seeing a [good] friend or relative whom one has not seen for a long time; he who becomes absorbed in that bliss can attain the mind reflective of that bliss.

In this, as in some other verses, the condition of the experience cannot be created; it has to occur on its own. When the existence of the condition — in this case, seeing a good friend after a long absence — is recognized, one has to concentrate, within seconds, all of the attention on the advancing flood of raw energy itself, while avoiding giving rise to derivatives of its manifestations.

जग्धिपानकृतोल्लासरसानन्दविजृम्भणात् ।
भावयेद्भरितावस्थां महानन्दस्ततो भवेत् ॥ ७२॥

jagdhipānakṛtollāsarasānandavijṛmbhaṇāt |
bhāvayedbharitāvasthāṃ mahānandastato bhavet || 72||

When eating and drinking makes one feel merry, [and "warm and fuzzy,"] and after the gradual spreading of the bliss that it caused to appear turns into the state of satiety; from that, a greater bliss might come. Dh. 49

When the feeling of satiety appears, one should maintain keen awareness, avoiding drowsiness or stupor and any block in *maṇipūra-cakra.*[59]

[59]See Appendix.

गितादिविषयास्वादासमसौख्यैकतात्मनः ।
योगिनस्तन्मयत्वेन मनोरूढेस्तदात्मता ॥ ७३ ॥

gitādiviṣayāsvādāsamasaukhyaikatātmanaḥ |
yoginastanmayatvena manorūḍhestadātmatā || *73*||

Dh. 50 [The moment after] experiencing the oneness of unequaled felicity resulting from savoring anything perceptible by the senses, like a song, [a beautiful curve, an enchanting dance,] etc., the yogi's [mind], being absorbed in that [felicity, relaxes into] the pure form of that [felicity]. The relaxation begins with, and is partially caused by, the ascent of the locus of control [to *sahasrāra-cakra*[60]].

Avoid any train of thought evoked by the felicity; be in the moment.

[60] See Appendix.

यत्र यत्र मनस्तुष्टिर्मनस्तत्रैव धारयेत् ।
तत्र तत्र परानन्दस्वरूपं सम्प्रवर्तते ॥ ७४ ॥

yatra yatra manastuṣṭirmanastatraiva dhārayet |
tatra tatra parānandasvarūpaṃ sampravartate || 74 ||

Wherever the mind finds contentment — if one were to maintain Dh. 51
the locus of control in that place, therein emerges the undiluted form of the ultimate bliss.

One should maintain attention on that particular fancy, idea, fantasy, or conception which brings mental contentment, while avoiding any elaborations on it or any actions, mental or physical; maintain full awareness. Make that "place" the center where-from the mind's eye observes the Universe.

If other thoughts or ideas appear, one should gently turn all attention back to same idea, fancy, etc., avoiding associative chains of thought. If dullness or sleepiness start setting in, one should raise his general alertness level. One should also avoid surges of *prāṇa* upwards through *iḍā* or *piṇgalā*.

अनागतायां निद्रायां प्रणष्टे बाह्यगोचरे ।
सावस्था मनसा गम्या परा देवी प्रकाशते ॥ ७५॥

anāgatāyāṃ nidrāyāṃ praṇaṣṭe bāhyagocare |
sāvasthā manasā gamyā parā devī prakāśate || 75||

Dh. 52 When the mind enters the state in between sleep and wakefulness, when external senses are lost [but awareness of internal stimuli remain], then *Śakti* is present in the *parā* state [and evinces the state of *bhairava*].

This state "in between sleep and wakefulness" frequently occurs after a couple of sleepless nights, when one tries to stay awake but exhaustion permeates the mind and the body. There is no need to do anything, just let the smoldering clusters of energy linger to indicate that which is beyond sleep and wakefulness.

तेजसा सूर्यदीपादेराकाशे शबलीकृते ।
दृष्टिर्निवेश्या तत्रैव स्वात्मरूपं प्रकाशते ॥ ७६ ॥

tejasā sūryadīpāderākāśe śabalīkṛte |
dṛṣṭirniveśyā tatraiva svātmarūpaṃ prakāśate || 76||

Having plunged the stare into an empty space where light of the sun, of a lamp, etc., is disappearing into the darkness in an indistinct manner, the reflection of one's soul appears therein. Dh. 53

Such empty space, where the light "is disappearing into the darkness in an indistinct manner," can be found in dark temples where light falls through small, high windows.

करण्किण्या क्रोधनया भैरव्या लेलिहानया ।
खेचर्या दृष्टिकाले च परावाप्तिः प्रकाशते ॥ ७७ ॥

karaṇkiṇyā krodhanayā bhairavyā lelihānayā |
khecaryā dṛṣṭikāle ca parāvāptiḥ prakāśate || 77 ||

Dh. 54 At the moment of beholding [with the mind's eye], brought about by means of *karaṅkiṇī*, or by means of *krodhanā*, or by means of *bhairavī*, or by means of *lelihānā*, or by means of *khecarī*, the attainment of the *śakti* in the *parā* state becomes evident.

Karaṅkiṇī, *krodhanā*, *bhairavī*, *lelihānā*, and *khecarī* are *mudrā*-s.

It should be noted that this is the most obscure verse of all in this text. Since an exact description of the *mudrā*-s is not available, what follows is an attempt at reconstructing the original meaning.

The nature of *mudrā* is that of reflection.[61]

A *mudrā* is a special configuration of *tattva*-s, or a mental construct, that creates a "closed circuit" or a "cocoon" that prevents the energy of potentiality from expressing itself in customary ways. It seals[62] off an inner chamber with the mind dwelling inside it.

A *mudrā* might be made with a particular tension in some muscles, or with a concentration of attention on specific sensations and images, or through a combination of both.

If upper[63] *cakra*-s[64] are unobstructed, then the locked energy of attention might lead to an excitation of the pituitary gland and to the perception of proprioceptive signals from it by the mind's eye (that is, the proprioceptive stimuli from the pituitary gland will be available to introspection).[65] The moment of this perception is "the moment of beholding" this verse talks about. Continued absorption into these proprioceptive flows of stimulation leads one to the edge of the *bhairava* state.

Karaṅkiṇī is described in verse 34; *krodhanā*, in 37.

---

[61] *mudrā ca pratibimbātmā* TA.32.1.b

[62] Lit. *mudrā* is any stamp or print or mark or impression.

[63] Those above the throat; at least six are mentioned in the scriptures.

[64] See Appendix.

[65] This is a highly speculative interpretation of the experience, since no objective information about the pituitary gland was available during my experience.

Bhairavī mudrā is described in the commentary to *sūtra* 18 of *Pratyabhijñāhṛdayam*: "Attention is concentrated on an internal object, but sense organs are fully open to external objects, while keeping one's open eyes from winking or wandering."[66]

Khecarī mudrā is described in *Haṭhayogapradīpikā*, Ch.3, thus:

> One should close, with the tip of the tongue, the opening in the skull, called *vyoma-cakra*,[67] and fix the gaze on the *ājña-cakra*. This will become *khecarī-mudrā*.[68] It should be held for about 24 minutes. The difficulty in practicing *khecarī-mudrā* is that it requires a lengthy process of making the tongue long enough to reach the *vyoma-cakra*; and it is not recommended, since there are other ways to attain the same effect.

What *lelihānā mūdrā* is, is less clear.

In all of the *mudrā*-s mentioned, it is important to maintain subtle attention on the central area of the skull.

[66] *antarlakṣyo bahirdṛṣṭiḥ nimeṣonmeṣavarjitaḥ*

[67] It is located at the top of the soft palate.

[68] *kapālakuhare jihvā praviṣṭā viparītagā | bhruvorantargatā dṛṣṭirmudrā bhavati khecarī || 32||*

मृद्वासने स्फिजैकेन हस्तपादौ निराश्रयम् ।
निधाय तत्प्रसण्गेन परा पूर्णा मतिर्भवेत् ॥ ७८ ॥

mṛdvāsane sphijaikena hastapādau nirāśrayam |
nidhāya tatprasaṇgena parā pūrṇā matirbhavet || 78||

Dh. 55 Sit on a soft [and high] cushion with one buttock, having lowered hands and feet so that they become without any support. By adherence to that [pose], the mental gesture can become utterly complete.

The posture should be in between standing and sitting. The mental gesture mentioned here is the one that maintains this finely balanced, but easily disturbed, posture.

उपविश्यासने सम्यग्बाहू कृत्वा अर्धकुञ्चितौ ।
कक्षव्योम्नि मनः कुर्वञ् शममायाति तल्लयात् ॥ ७९ ॥

upaviśyāsane samyagbāhū kṛtvā ardhakuñcitau |
kakṣavyomni manaḥ kurvañ śamamāyāti tallayāt || 79||

While sitting in an *āsana*,[69] having both arms [extended upwards and] half-bent, directing all attention into the both armpits, one moves towards tranquility through dissolution of the mind. Dh. 56

Hands should not touch each other. Attention should be distributed equally into both armpits. Maintain a straight back, keeping the posture as comfortable and effortless as possible.

[69] A yoga posture.

स्थूलरूपस्य भावस्य स्तब्धां दृष्टिं निपात्य च ।
अचिरेण निराधारं मनः कृत्वा शिवं व्रजेत् ॥ ८० ॥

sthūlarūpasya bhāvasya stabdhāṃ dṛṣṭiṃ nipātya ca |
acireṇa nirādhāraṃ manaḥ kṛtvā śivaṃ vrajet || 80||

Dh. 57 By casting down a stare that was immovably fixed on a solid object [for some time], [and thus] having instantaneously taken away the support the mind's eye had [while one was looking at the object], one might wander into [the state of] being *śiva*.

मध्यजिह्वे स्फारितास्ये मध्ये निक्षिप्य चेतनाम् ।
होच्चारं मनसा कुर्वंस्ततः शान्ते प्रलीयते ॥ ८१॥

madhyajihve sphāritāsye madhye nikṣipya cetanām |
hoccāraṃ manasā kurvaṃstataḥ śānte pralīyate || 81||

With mouth wide open and the tongue suspended in the middle of it, one should throw the mind into the middle of the tongue and mentally utter *ha*; then the mind becomes dissolved into tranquility.

"Mentally uttering the sound *ha*" means that the voice apparatus is configured for actual utterance, but no sound is produced. The sound *ha* is like English *huh* with no breath at the end and a short vowel. Dh. 58

आसने शयने स्थित्वा निराधारं विभावयन् ।
स्वदेहं मनसि क्षीणे क्षणात्क्षीणाशयो भवेत् ॥ ८२॥

āsane śayane sthitvā nirādhāraṃ vibhāvayan |
svadehaṃ manasi kṣīṇe kṣaṇātkṣīṇāśayo bhavet || 82||

Dh. 59 If, while remaining in a laying-down *āsana*, one were to imagine one's own body to be supportless, then, when attention is waning, one's habitual mental dispositions would instantly lose their strength.

Here, "to imagine the body to be supportless" one has to spread attention equally, first over joints, then over the fingers and toes of both hands and feet, and then over the whole surface of the body.

चलासने स्थितस्याथ शनैर्वा देहचालनात् ।
प्रशान्ते मानसे भावे देवि दिव्यौघमाप्नुयात् ॥ ८३॥

calāsane sthitasyātha śanairvā dehacālanāt |
praśānte mānase bhāve devi divyaughamāpnuyāt || 83||

When sitting on a shaking seat [such as on a horse, in a moving train], the swaying movements of the body gradually become mentally allayed. O Devi, the flood of spontaneity is within reach. Dh. 60

This works similarly to the technique from verse 43. In old times it was practiced while traveling on top of an elephant. Riding a camel, slow walking horse, or taking a train ride on an old bumpy rail-track might work as well. When the body is swaying, let it and let the mind follow it instead of attempting to maintain an immovable head posture.

आकाशं विमलं पश्यन्कृत्वा दृष्टिं निरन्तराम् ।
स्तब्धात्मा तत्क्षणाद्देवि भैरवं वपुराप्नुयात् ॥ ८४ ॥

ākāśaṃ vimalaṃ paśyankṛtvā dṛṣṭiṃ nirantarām |
stabdhātmā tatkṣaṇāddevi bhairavaṃ vapurāpnuyāt || 84 ||

Dh. 61 He who, while staring at the spotless sky, makes the gaze uninterrupted [that is, without intervening thoughts or looking elsewhere or winking], and who at the same time stops the breath, O *Devī* — he might bring the *bhairava* form within the reach.

Here, the expression "within reach" means that the state of *bhairava* is not caused or conditioned by anything, but that it occurs spontaneously. Any technique is only capable of effecting a state of consciousness where this spontaneity is likely to actualize.

लीनं मूर्ध्नि वियत्सर्वं भैरवत्वेन भावयेत् ।
तत्सर्वं भैरवाकारतेजस्तत्त्वं समाविशेत् ॥ ८५॥

līnaṃ mūrdhni viyatsarvaṃ bhairavatvena bhāvayet |
tatsarvaṃ bhairavākāratejastattvaṃ samāviśet || 85||

If one were to cause everything [that appears to the mind] to dissolve apart in the forehead, using the natural tendency [of ideas and impressions] to fade away, then one might become immersed into the all-pervading luminosity, appearing as limitless formless spatiality. Dh. 62

Keep your eyes closed and concentrate on the place between the brows (*ājña-cakra*[70]). Whenever an idea, image, impression, sensation, etc. arises, look at it by seeing it in *ājña-cakra* with full attention, without diverting it to associations evoked by that idea, image, etc. Due to concentration without associations, that idea, image, etc. will begin to fade. Let it. When the next idea, image, etc. arises, do the same. With time, the inner space, which is like a screen on which all these ideas, images, etc. appear, will become filled with shapeless, limitless brilliance. The state of *bhairava* is close.

[70] See Appendix.

किञ्चिज्ज्ञातं द्वैतदायि बाह्यालोकस्तमः पुनः ।
विश्वादि भैरवं रूपं ज्ञात्वानन्तप्रकाशभृत् ॥ ८६ ॥

kiñcijjñātaṃ dvaitadāyi bāhyālokastamaḥ punaḥ |
viśvādi bhairavaṃ rūpaṃ jñātvānantaprakāśabhṛt || 86||

Dh. 63 Whatever experience bestowing duality, be it external light or darkness, or the waking state [or the dreaming state, or the deep sleep state], having been understood as a [particularization of the pure] form of *bhairava*, [one might enter the state] bearing infinite light.

Here, "having been understood as a [particularization of the pure] form *bhairava*" means "resolved into a particular configuration of *tattva*-s." To do this, it is helpful to observe transitions between the wakeful state and dreaming state, between the dreaming state and deep sleep, and between bright light and total darkness.

एवमेव दुर्निशायां कृष्णपक्षागमे चिरम् ।
तैमिरं भावयन्रूपं भैरवं रूपमेष्यति ॥ ८७॥

evameva durniśāyāṃ kṛṣṇapakṣāgame ciram |
taimiraṃ bhāvayanrūpaṃ bhairavaṃ rūpameṣyati || 87||

Verily, one who, during a gloomy, moonless night of the darkest phase of the moon, [contemplates the darkness] for a long time [and] sees the pure image of the darkness itself will go towards the state of *bhairava*. Dh. 64

This is a specialization of the practice from verse 67. Staring into complete darkness for a long time results in abandoning the visual modality of perception and, as Jaideva Singh put it, "one is filled with a sense of awe and uncanny mystery, and easily slips into the mystic consciousness." [Sin03b]

एवमेव निमील्यादौ नेत्रे कृष्णाभमग्रतः ।
प्रसार्य भैरवं रूपं भावयंस्तन्मयो भवेत् ॥ ८८ ॥

evameva nimīlyādau netre kṛṣṇābhamagrataḥ |
prasārya bhairavaṃ rūpaṃ bhāvayaṃstanmayo bhavet || *88*||

Dh. 65 Similarly [to the previous verse], at the moment of closing one's eyes, the darkness spreads as if flowing from somewhere in front of the eyes. He who is evoking the *bhairava* form [in this way] might become as if made of it [the darkness, that is].

Swami Lakshman Joo comments that after closing one's eyes one has to meditate on the darkness. The meditation is complete if upon opening one's eyes, one still sees at first nothing but darkness. This should be tried inside a dimly lit room, so that closing one's eyelids results in seeing only darkness.

यस्य कस्येन्द्रियस्यापि व्याघाताच्च निरोधतः ।
प्रविष्टस्याद्वये शून्ये तत्रैव आत्मा प्रकाशते ॥ ८९ ॥

yasya kasyendriyasyāpi vyāghātācca nirodhataḥ |
praviṣṭasyādvaye śūnye tatraiva ātmā prakāśate || 89||

Having entered into non-dual emptiness, occurring when a sense organ is first agitated and then is deprived of variability of stimulation, therein the Self becomes manifest. Dh. 66

This technique is a generalization of the one presented in verse 88.

Look at a uniform, one-color, unchangeable visual field, or listen to one pure tone, etc. There appears to be a gap between the stimuli and its impression on the mind. The mind will try to restore the direct connection — to make a bridge across this gap — and in consequence of this, the perception will be as if vibrating. Let go of the effort to reconnect with the stimuli. The gap illuminates the reality beyond.

Swami Lakshman Joo's interpretation of this verse is "to meditate on the incipient sensation of pain when accidentally striking a limb or an organ of sense with an object."

अबिन्दुमविसर्गं चाकारं जपतो महान् ।
उदेति देवि सहसा ज्ञानौघः परमेश्वरः ॥ ९० ॥

abindumavisargaṃ cākāraṃ japato mahān |
udeti devi sahasā jñānaughaḥ parameśvaraḥ || 90||

Dh. 67 By muttering *a*-sound without *ṃ* and without *ḥ*, there suddenly arises, O *Devī*, [the state of] the ultimate commander, abundant with knowledge.

Swami Lakshman Joo says in the commentary to this verse that the *a* sound here (pronounced as English short vowel in *sun*) should be short, with the mouth as if open with astonishment. The sound itself is whispered and is as if uttered by the the movement of opening the mouth. It is without nasalization of *ṃ* and without the echo of *ḥ*. (See commentary to verse 30 for explanatioins what sounds are denoted with *ṃ* and *ḥ*.)

It helps to place the mind's eye on top of the skull.

वर्णस्य सविसर्गस्य विसर्गान्तं चितिं कुरु ।
निराधारेण चित्तेन स्पृशेद्ब्रह्म सनातनम् ॥ ९१॥

varṇasya savisargasya visargāntaṃ citiṃ kuru |
nirādhāreṇa cittena spṛśedbrahma sanātanam || 91||

Fix attention on the end of the *visarga* of any syllable ending with *visarga*. Then, by the mind devoid of any support frame, you may touch the everlasting Brahman. Dh. 68

Any syllable ending with *visarga* (like *maḥ*, *taḥ*, *vaḥ*) may be used. For how to pronounce the sounds, see comments to verse 30.

व्योमाकारं स्वमात्मानं ध्यायेद्दिग्भिरनावृतम् ।
निराश्रया चितिः शक्तिः स्वरूपं दर्शयेत्तदा ॥ ९२॥

vyomākāraṃ svamātmānaṃ dhyāyeddigbhiranāvṛtam |
nirāśrayā citiḥ śaktiḥ svarūpaṃ darśayettadā || 92||

Dh. 69 If one were to meditate on one's own self as a vast sky, limitless in all directions, then one would see the power to amplify/attenuate attention, devoid of all sensory and mental images, patterns, memories, etc., as one's own true nature.

Here, "attention" means the general process of amplification/attenuation/selection of active or to-become-active mental entities.

किंचिदङ्गं विभिद्यादौ तीक्ष्णसूच्यादिना ततः ।
तत्रैव चेतनां युक्त्वा भैरवे निर्मला गतिः ॥ ९३ ॥

kiṃcidaṅgaṃ vibhidyādau tīkṣṇasūcyādinā tataḥ |
tatraiva cetanāṃ yuktvā bhairave nirmalā gatiḥ || *93* ||

Having pierced any limb with the tip of a sharp needle, etc., and then having concentrated undivided attention upon that [sensation of pain]; [this is] a pure way into [the state of] *bhairava.* Dh. 70

It is the very intensity of the pain that is put into the context of no action/no reaction to it. The pure awareness of this pain leads the mind to the state of *bhairava.*

चित्ताद्यन्तःकृतिर्नास्ति ममान्तर्भावयेदिति ।
विकल्पानामभावेन विकल्पैरुज्झितो भवेत् ॥ ९४॥

cittādyantaḥkṛtirnāsti mamāntarbhāvayediti |
vikalpānāmabhāvena vikalpairujjhito bhavet || *94* ||

Dh. 71 Contemplating thus: "Inner activities, such as the flow of associations, inner speech, [aspirations of ego, desires of flesh,] etc., are not [happening] inside *me*," one would become devoid of *vikalpa*-s (polarizations) by virtue of them being inactive.

All internal activities that one notices should be contemplated upon in this way. Thoughts, feelings, actual pain (if any), breathing, intentions, desires, aversions, speech production, speech comprehension, facial expressions, hunger, mental gestures, that which contemplates — according to this verse, everything that one notices — should be perceived as "not happening inside of me."

माया विमोहिनी नाम कलायाः कलनं स्थितम् ।
इत्यादिधर्मं तत्त्वानां कलयन्न पृथग्भवेत् ॥ ९५॥

māyā vimohinī nāma kalāyāḥ kalanaṃ sthitam |
ityādidharmaṃ tattvānāṃ kalayanna pṛthagbhavet || 95||

Māyā avoids being manifested by the constant incitement of *kalā*-s. Dh. 72

The incitement is caused by selective masking of conditions that determine the relevancy of *kalā*-s activation, thus leaving dominant only desire/action aspects. Because of the consequences of this incitement, *Māyā* is called bewildering.

He who observes thus the primary foundation of [all] *tattva*-s [below *māyā*] does not remain fragmented in his own self.

Māyā clothes the terrifying beauty of naked reality in order to make it palatable to the self-limiting Ego.

Notice how micro-skills fire all the time. The sounds of a human voice triggers speech recognition. The image of a human face activates the reading of emotions expressed on that face. Printed letters — reading a text. Morsels of food — thoughts of cooking or eating. A computer screen — the impulse to browse the Internet. All such micro-skills channel attention into pre-established grooves of activity. These are examples of *kalā*-s.

The channeled flows of energy are protected by the five armors: *kalā-tattva*, *vidyā-tattva*, *rāga-tattva*, *niyati-tattva*, and *kāla-tattva*. (Read entries for these five armors in the "Concepts" section.)

The practice of analyzing the stability of habitual grooves of behavior and the systematic loosening of the armors with the purpose of unlearning that behavior, leads not only to experiencing the state of *bhairava*, but towards yoga.

The practice consists of four steps, used iteratively. First, identify a behavior that is personally significant and limiting. To do this step it helps to follow advice of Francis Bacon, "Write down the thoughts of the moment. Those that come unsought for are commonly the most valuable."

Second, find out how the armors protect the shape and activation of this behavior. Third, prove to yourself that the armors are irrational and based either on ignorance or habit. And finally, resolve to engage the new understanding in daily life.

In order to perform the third step, one might need to apply this very practice to a particular armor, considering it as a behavior for the first step.

झगितीच्छां समुत्पन्नामवलोक्य शमं नयेत् ।
यत एव समुद्भूता ततस्तत्रैव लीयते ॥ ९६॥

jhagitīcchāṃ samutpannāmavalokya śamaṃ nayet |
yata eva samudbhūtā tatastatraiva līyate || 96||

If one were to allay a desire, as soon as one noticed that it had arisen, then it would be dissolved into the place from which it was born. Dh. 73

To dissolve a desire, one needs first to dissolve the tension of the intent to pursue the desire; then, just observe the desire, while preventing it from spawning plans, proximities, associations, mental attitudes, etc.

A desire should not be suppressed; rather, it should be allowed to manifest and then be observed to subside in the same way it arose.

यदा ममेच्छा नोत्पन्ना ज्ञानं वा कस्तदास्मि वै ।
तत्त्वतोऽहं तथाभूतस्तल्लीनस्तन्मना भवेत् ॥ ९७॥

yadā mamecchā notpannā jñānaṃ vā kastadāsmi vai |
tattvato'haṃ tathābhūtastallīnastanmanā bhavet || 97||

Dh. 74 "When my desires do not spring up, nor any perceptions, what then am I? Truly I am non-existent when that happens." If one were to become absorbed into that [state evoked by the mental gesture "no desires, no experiencing"], then one's *manas* would become non-existent.

Of course, a "no desires, no experiencing" mental gesture should encompass the desire to enter the state of *bhairava* and the observing of entering that state. It is essential to give up results of this practice before starting it.

इच्छायामथवा ज्ञाने जाते चित्तं निवेशयेत् ।
आत्मबुद्ध्यानन्यचेतास्ततस्तत्त्वार्थदर्शनम् ॥ ९८ ॥

icchāyāmathavā jñāne jāte cittaṃ niveśayet |
ātmabuddhyānanyacetāstatastattvārthadarśanam || 98||

If one were to immerse the mind into [just] arisen desire or into [just] emerged experience, then he who minds nothing else [but that desire or experience], by being aware [at the same time] of one's own breath, would come to contemplation of the [*śiva-*]*tattva.* Dh. 75

Just when you notice arising of desire, immerse the mind into that desire completely. If thoughts connected with fulfilling the desire start branching out — you are making plans, etc. — then the immersion is only partial. The attention should be in the desire as an inner movement (that is, as a specific movement of one's thought).

Along with the immersion, one should have the awareness of one's own breath in the fashion of vipassana practice — being aware of breathing in and of breathing out. Here is a fine point: awareness can exist along with mindfulness. Therefore, immersing one's mind completely into one thing does not contradict being fully aware, at the same time, of any other thing. This concurrence, though, requires some practice.

When both the full immersion of the mind into the desire and the awareness of one's breath are present, one will find himself to be drifting into the contemplation of something. And that something is *śiva-tattva.* This drift, if uninterrupted, brings one to the edge of the state of *bhairava.*

Instead of a desire, one can use an intense experience. The desire or the experience used should have enough intensity to capture one's attention.

निर्निमित्तं भवेज्ज्ञानं निराधारं भ्रमात्मकम् ।
tattvataḥ kasyacinnaitadevaṃ bhāvī śivaḥ priye || 99||

nirnimittaṃ bhavejjñānaṃ nirādhāraṃ bhramātmakam |
tattvataḥ kasyacinnaitadevaṃ bhāvī śivaḥ priye || 99||

Dh. 76 One who is contemplating thus: "Cognition that is without a motive or goal, that is without any support [to provide stability, such as an image, idea, sensation, etc.], or that is chaotic — truly, such cognition is a cognition of nothing whatsoever," becomes *Śiva*, O Dear!

Consider any idea or cognition that comes to mind. Was it caused by a desire? Does it reflect a state of the body? Is it shaped by an external stimuli? Is it based upon other ideas (in the same way any meaning of the sentence "self is illusory" is based on meanings of the words "self," "is," and "illusory")? Does it remain the same or change significantly when the context changes? Does it represent a goal or an intention?

Can you find any cognition such that none of the above questions has a "yes" answer? If any one question has a "yes" answer, what would happen to the cognition if the cause, the goal, the support, or the context disappeared? Keep contemplating in this fashion and you can become aware of the basis of all cognitions.

Jaideva Singh formulates this contemplation thus: "All knowledge is without cause, without base and deceptive. From the point of view of absolute Reality, this knowledge does not belong to any person."

चिद्धर्मा सर्वदेहेषु विशेषो नास्ति कुत्रचित् ।
अतश्च तन्मयं सर्वं भावयन्भवजिज्जनः ॥ १००॥

ciddharmā sarvadeheṣu viśeṣo nāsti kutracit |
ataśca tanmayaṃ sarvaṃ bhāvayanbhavajijjanaḥ || 100||

He who contemplates thus: "The infrastructure of consciousness is the same for all [sentient beings]; thence [the consciousness of] each [sentient being] is, in essence, one and the same consciousness," conquers the continuity of becoming. Dh. 77

"Becoming" here is the link in the twelve-fold chain of causation (see *Paṭiccasamuppādasutta* SN XII.1).

It is understood that though the infrastructure of consciousness is the same, the content of consciousness might be different. Thus, the variety of behaviors is explained by the variety of contents, and the variety of contents is understood to be a result of the Divine Play.

"The infrastructure of consciousness" is understood to be the general mechanisms, structures, and features of mental activities in sentient beings. For example, excitation/inhibition, *tattva*-s, luminosity, self-will/inner spontaneity, long-term/short-term memory, interfaces with physiological infrastructure of the being, etc.

Jaideva Singh explains this formula as: "The same Self characterized by consciousness is present in all the bodies; there is no difference in it anywhere."

कामक्रोधलोभमोहमदमात्सर्यगोचरे ।
बुद्धिं निस्तिमितां कृत्वा तत्तत्त्वमवशिष्यते ॥ १०१॥

kāmakrodhalobhamohamadamātsaryagocare |
buddhiṃ nistimitāṃ kṛtvā tattattvamavaśiṣyate || *101* ||

Dh. 78 If one, being under the influence of love, anger, confusion, bewilderment, hilarity, or jealousy [or any other strong emotion], quiets the power of forming conceptions, then the *bhairava tattva* is left as the only dominant aspect.

An experience of a strong emotion might induce a rush of thoughts that frame, explain, compare, judge, alleviate, etc. that emotion. If one can quiet that rush and become saturated by the emotion, then that is the state where the *bhairava* aspect is predominant.

Swami Lakshman Joo points out that the rush should be quieted and the excitement should be transformed by steady awareness, not after the emotion has unfolded but as it is arising; and to be able to do that one needs to be broadminded — like a child.

Jaideva Singh describes the process thus:

> ... he should dissociate his mind from the object of the emotion and concentrate deeply on the emotion itself, without either accepting it or rejecting it. ... When he is thus intensely introverted, the passion becomes calmed like a charmed snake; all *vikalpa*-s are shed like leaves in autumn.

इन्द्रजालमयं विश्वं व्यस्तं वा चित्रकर्मवत् ।
भ्रमद्वा ध्यायतः सर्वम् पश्यतश्च सुखोद्गमः ॥ १०२॥

indrajālamayaṃ viśvaṃ vyastaṃ vā citrakarmavat |
bhramadvā dhyāyataḥ sarvam paśyataśca sukhodgamaḥ || 102||

"This world is an illusion [where the opposites transform into each other], or a painting, disintegrating [as one moves closer to it], or an ever-changing [mosaic of time frames and forms]." Meditating thus or observing everything in this way is an origin of happiness. Dh. 79

As Heraclitus wrote, "The same is Dionysus — in honor of whom they craze and celebrate — and Hades." Observing the world in such fashion requires analytical tools. It might be the atomism of Democritus, or the system of *tattva*-s, or anything that allows one to construct differing experiences from the same "blocks."

न चित्तं निक्षिपेद्दुःखे न सुखे वा परिक्षिपेत् ।
भैरवि ज्ञाय तां मध्ये किं तत्त्वमवशिष्यते ॥ १०३॥

na cittaṃ nikṣipedduḥkhe na sukhe vā parikṣipet |
bhairavi jñāyatāṃ madhye kiṃ tattvamavaśiṣyate || *103*||

Dh. 80 If one were to avoid plunging the mind into unhappiness, or distress, or feeling vulnerable, and also to avoid embracing happiness, comfort, or security, O Bhairavi, [and thus] to have experienced her, *śakti*, in the intermediate state, what *tattva* is left as a residue [of that experience]?

Daniel Odier interprets this verse as,

> O Bhairavi, do not reside in pleasure or in pain; instead, be constantly in the ineffable spatial reality that links them.

विहाय निजदेहास्थां सर्वत्रास्मीति भावयन् ।
दृढेन मनसा दृष्ट्या नान्येक्षिण्या सुखी भवेत् ॥ १०४॥

vihāya nijadehāsthāṃ sarvatrāsmīti bhāvayan |
dṛḍhena manasā dṛṣṭyā nānyekṣiṇyā sukhī bhavet || 104||

"Abandoning concerns over the body given [to me] at birth, I am everywhere." Contemplating thus, with mental gaze beholding nothing else, one will become happy. Dh. 81

When a care for your own body presents itself, disregard it immediately. Contemplate "I am not my body and I am not confined by it — I am everywhere." Focus on this contemplation only.

Should you feel a mental barrier between your own body or your own self and the Universe, ask yourself, "Do I perceive the Universe, act in it, feel it, only because it is the means to serve my own body? Is not the Universe fascinating enough that I might be curious about it for no utilitarian purpose? Are not the sharp boundaries I perceive between myself and the outside world introduced into the picture by the habit of making the body comfortable?"

The body has a wonderful ability to take care of itself, to sedate pains, to adjust to an inconvenient posture, to find the inner energy to deal with hunger, etc. — so let it.

Also, see verse 100.

घटादौ यच्च विज्ञानमिच्छाद्यं वा ममान्तरे ।
नैव सर्वगतं जातं भावयन्निति सर्वगः ॥ १०५॥

ghaṭādau yacca vijñānamicchādyaṃ vā mamāntare |
naiva sarvagataṃ jātaṃ bhāvayaniti sarvagaḥ || 105||

Dh. 82 What is recognized in [an image of] a jar, etc., or a desire, etc., is inside me. What is all-pervading is neither born nor caused. Contemplating thus, one becomes all-pervading.

A distinction is made between things as perceived "outside" (like objects — a jar, a rock, the sun, etc.) vs. "inside" (like desires, feelings, etc.). Contemplate this distinction as being projected onto a perceptual plane, and that that plane is "inside"; so the distinction "inside/outside" is not inherent. (Good examples to contemplate are errors of perception, like Freudian slips and hallucinations.) Think about the fact that any "outside" thing can be seen as vividly in a dream. The basis of the perception and cognition is the same, whether it is a cognition of an "external" object or of an "internal" desire. This basis is pervading everything one is capable of perceiving or imagining or cognizing.

ग्राह्यग्राहकसंवित्तिः सामान्या सर्वदेहिनाम् ।
योगिनां तु विशेषोऽस्ति सम्बन्धे सावधानता ॥ १०६॥

grāhyagrāhakasaṃvittiḥ sāmānyā sarvadehinām |
yogināṃ tu viśeṣo'sti sambandhe sāvadhānatā || 106||

The sense that there is what is to be perceived, and a point of view from which it is perceived, is common to all embodied souls; the distinction of a yogi is the attentiveness to the relation [between the two].

This is not a practice. It is a commentary on the previous verse.

The continual awareness of how the perception is being shaped by "what is to be perceived" and "a point of view from which it is perceived" is the point of this verse. Everyone can think in terms of the distinction "objective/subjective," while yogis can think from the place in between these two.

स्ववदन्यशरीरेऽपि संवित्तिमनुभावयेत् ।
अपेक्षां स्वशरीरस्य त्यक्त्वा व्यापी दिनैर्भवेत् ॥ १०७॥

svavadanyaśarīre'pi saṃvittimanubhāvayet |
apekṣāṃ svaśarīrasya tyaktvā vyāpī dinairbhavet || 107||

Dh. 83 If one were to sense [in one's own mind and body] or feel [in one's own mind and body] the body of another, as if it were one's own, then, having abandoned any reference of or consideration towards one's own body, one would become "all-pervading" in a matter of several days.

निराधारं मनः कृत्वा विकल्पान्न विकल्पयेत् ।
तदात्मपरमात्मत्वे भैरवो मृगलोचने ॥ १०८ ॥

nirādhāraṃ manaḥ kṛtvā vikalpānna vikalpayet |
tadātmaparamātmatve bhairavo mṛgalocane || 108||

If, having made *manas* frame-less, one were to avoid contriving any vikalpa-s, then [the state of] *bhairava* would be in the naked core of one's own self, O Gazelle-eyed one! Dh. 84

"Frame-less" here means "without anything that allows the mind to continuously build frames of reference, patterns of engagement, etc."

Ego is eager to find a pair of opposites in which to establish itself through sticking to one and opposing the other. When Ego is threatened, it evokes continual judgment of "this is good" or "this is bad" on a variety of values. One should become aware of this tendency as well as of any *vikalpa*-s which are predominant in one's psyche, and should dissolve attempts to contrive *vikalpa*-s; for example, it can be done by using "dependent co-arising" analysis (see [Sem08], commentary to *sūtra* 8). Any "values" should be let go of, at least temporarily, and one should meditate on the Void.

सर्वज्ञः सर्वकर्ता च व्यापकः परमेश्वरः ।
स एवाहं शैवधर्मा इति दार्ढ्याच्छिवो भवेत् ॥ १०९॥

sarvajñaḥ sarvakartā ca vyāpakaḥ parameśvaraḥ |
sa evāhaṃ śaivadharmā iti dārḍhyācchivo bhavet || 109||

Dh. 85 "All-experiencing One, the creator of everything, the One who pervades everything, the ultimate commander, *Śiva* is indeed. I am endowed with all his qualities." Being firm [in asserting this], one becomes *śiva.*

A firm assertion of the maxim "all-experiencing One,..." requires putting it to practice. One needs to get rid of *āṇavamala,* at the very least.

Jaideva Singh comments that assertion expressed in this verse is a direct first step to self-recognition as *Śiva* — the way of the *Pratyabhijñā* system (see [Sem08] for detail of the system).

जलस्येवोर्मयो वह्नेर्ज्वालाभण्ग्यः प्रभा रवेः ।
ममैव भैरवस्यैता विश्वभङ्गो विभेदिताः ॥ ११० ॥

jalasyevormayo vahnerjvālābhaṇgyaḥ prabhā raveḥ |
mamaiva bhairavasyaitā viśvabhaṅgyo vibheditāḥ || 110||

The waves of water, the flames of fire that have broken off, the rays of sun — all these are mine, indeed, *Bhairava*'s; whatever is to be broken off or separated [are all about to dissolve into me]. Dh. 86

This is not so much a particular technique, but a template for creating your own. The meaning is that whatever becomes detached and unsupported by *aparā-śakti* merges back into the pure form of *bhairava.*

Jaideva Singh gives a different interpretation and comments that this assertion is a direct second step to self-recognition as *śiva* — the way of the *Pratyabhijñā* system. Swami Lakshman Joo explains, "As waves and tides are one with water, and the tongues of all flames are one with fire, and as rays are one with the sun, in the same way, all the universal currents rise from me, who is one with *Bhairava.*"

भ्रान्त्वा भ्रान्त्वा शरीरेण त्वरितं भुवि पातनात् ।
क्षोभशक्तिविरामेण परा संजायते दशा ॥ १११॥

bhrāntvā bhrāntvā śarīreṇa tvaritaṃ bhuvi pātanāt |
kṣobhaśaktivirāmeṇa parā saṃjāyate daśā || 111||

Dh. 87 Having roamed around [the forest till exhaustion so that one has to exhort oneself to go on], from falling with the whole body at once on the ground simultaneously with the suspension of the ability to become agitated, the ultimate condition takes place.

One can wander through rooms of a big art museum, instead of a forest. The point is that there are three requirements for the activity. The first is — there is no goal to reach and no plan to follow. The second — there is a variety of perceptual stimuli. The third — one is physically exhausted and lacking in willpower.

Then, collapse and abandon it all.

Another interpretation, given by Jaideva Singh, is that one has to whirl his body around and around until the control of the body is lost; then let it swiftly fall down on the ground.

आधारेष्वथवाऽशक्त्याऽज्ञानाच्चित्तलयेन वा ।
जातशक्तिसमावेशक्षोभान्ते भैरवं वपुः ॥ ११२॥

ādhāreṣvathavā'śaktyā'jñānāccittalayena vā |
jātaśaktisamāveśakṣobhānte bhairavaṃ vapuḥ || 112||

When the end of agitation, brought about by an absorption into Dh. 88
energized potentiality [occurs], whether through absence of energy to support the barriers of cognition, or by dissolution caused by the lack of cognizance of something in the attention focus, the state of *bhairava* [happens].

This verse gives a general schema of circumstances, particular instances of which are described in the previous verse and in verses 37 and 101.

Another example would be the intense pondering over a koan or over a paradox.

Swami Lakshman Joo explains this verse thus: If one wants to see but the eyes can't see, if one wants to know but the mind can't comprehend, then only the pure curiosity remains. When that happens, become absorbed in that curiosity and the mind will melt into its natural state.

संप्रदायमिमं देवि शृणु सम्यग्वदाम्यहम् ।
कैवल्यं जायते सद्यो नेत्रयोः स्तब्धमात्रयोः ॥ ११३॥

saṃpradāyamimaṃ devi śṛṇu samyagvadāmyaham |
kaivalyaṃ jāyate sadyo netrayoḥ stabdhamātrayoḥ || *113*||

Dh. 89 Hear, O *Devī*, this technique, transmitted from one teacher to another. I will tell it in its entirety.

The perfect detachment is born at once from mere immobility of both eyes.

"Immobility" means the lack of any movement of the physical eyes. It might be effected by closing the eyes and applying a slight pressure to them in the front.

संकोचं कर्णयोः कृत्वा ह्यधोद्वारे तथैव च ।
अनच्कमहलं ध्यायन्विशेद्ब्रह्म सनातनम् ॥ ११४॥

saṃkocaṃ karṇayoḥ kṛtvā hyadhodvāre tathaiva ca |
anackamahalaṃ dhyāyanviśedbrahma sanātanam || *114* ||

Having compressed both ears [with gentle pressure of a finger of each hand] and, similarly, [having compressed] the two gates below, he who meditates on [a sound having] no vowels and no consonants might enter the everlasting Brahman. Dh. 90

The two gates below are the anus and the root of the penis. They are compressed by gentle pressure of the heels that are placed against them when one assumes *siddhāsana.* The heels should be placed in such a manner that the pressure on the bones on both sides is equal (see pp.582-587 of [Cou01] for details). The purpose of both compressions is to influence distribution of the *apāna.*

The sound to be listened for appears on its own, deep inside, with no particular place of origin noticeable. Have no intention to hear the sound, or the tension might interfere with the setup.

कूपादिके महागर्ते स्थित्वोपरि निरीक्षणात् ।
अविकल्पमतेः सम्यक्सद्यश्चित्तलयः स्फुटम् ॥ ११५॥

kūpādike mahāgarte sthitvopari nirīkṣaṇāt |
avikalpamateḥ samyaksadyaścittalayaḥ sphuṭam || 115||

Dh. 91 When standing above a deep well, chasm, etc., or in front of a dark cave, at the moment the thought becomes devoid of polarizations from looking inside it, dissolution of *manas* [occurs] — that is certain.

Daniel Odier give this interpretation: "At the edge of a well, gaze motionless into its depth until wonder seizes you and merge into space."

यत्र यत्र मनो याति बाह्ये वाभ्यन्तरेऽपि वा ।
तत्र तत्र शिवावास्था व्यापकत्वात्क्व यास्यति ॥ ११६ ॥

yatra yatra mano yāti bāhye vābhyantare'pi vā |
tatra tatra śivāvāsthā vyāpakatvātkva yāsyati || 116||

Wherever mind flees — whether to something internal or external — there and then the state of *śiva* [manifests itself]. Where can one escape its pervasiveness? Dh. 92

Observe where your mind is absorbed and how it escapes from that absorption. When the mind wanders, it is the transitions that reveal the *śiva-tattva.* In this very act of detachment, which allows a change of the locus of absorption, the fundamental nature of the mind manifests itself.

यत्र यत्र अक्षमार्गेण चैतन्यं व्यज्यते विभोः ।
तस्य तन्मात्रधर्मित्वाच्चिल्लयाद्भरितात्मता ॥ ११७॥

yatra yatra akṣamārgeṇa caitanyaṃ vyajyate vibhoḥ |
tasya tanmātradharmitvāccillayādbharitātmatā || 117||

Dh. 93 Wherever, by the trajectory of sensory perception, the consciousness is driven away from its pervasive quality of being rigidly framed by modalities of perception; therein, from dissolving into the pure perceptive attention,[71] the consciousness reverts to that Self which lacks nothing, that is complete and whole.

When the opportunity to transcend a modality of perception occurs, just observe, having no expectations, no intentions, and no fears.

[71] *cit*

क्षुताद्यन्ते भये शोके गह्वरे वा रणाद्द्रुते ।
कुतूहले क्षुधाद्यन्ते ब्रह्मसत्तामयी दशा ॥ ११८ ॥

kṣutādyante bhaye śoke gahvare vā raṇāddrute |
kutūhale kṣudhādyante brahmasattāmayī daśā || 118||

At the beginning and the end of sneezing, when utterly afraid, full of anguish, in the midst of confusion,[72] when feeling as if melted with pleasure, when becoming curious, or at the beginning and the end of feeling hungry, [there is] that state that is full of the actuality of Brahman.[73] Dh. 94

One should keep attention and awareness on the events mentioned. For example, try being fully aware of and attentive to all the stages of sneezing. Then the state of *bhairava* is close to emerging.

[72]The sort of confusion that Zen koans attempt to invoke.
[73]Infinite plasticity and all-pervasive spontaneity.

वस्तुषु स्मर्यमाणेषु दृष्टे देशे मनस्त्यजेत् ।
स्वशरीरं निराधारं कृत्वा प्रसरति प्रभुः ॥ ११९ ॥

vastuṣu smaryamāṇeṣu dṛṣṭe deśe manastyajet |
svaśarīraṃ nirādhāraṃ kṛtvā prasarati prabhuḥ || 119||

Dh. 95 If one were to leave the mind wandering in some vividly recollected place, and having thus removed support from his own subtle body, then the state of change from tension to flow spreads [like a shadow from the setting sun].

That sudden change from the tension and rigidity of self-guarding Ego to the flow of the Beyond might develop into boundless spatiality of air and the universal transmutability of fire. Then the Luminous Void dawns.

क्वचिद्वस्तुनि विन्यस्य शनैर्दृष्टिं निवर्तयेत् ।
तज्ज्ञानं चित्तसहितं देवि शून्यालायो भवेत् ॥ १२० ॥

kvacidvastuni vinyasya śanairdṛṣṭiṃ nivartayet |
tajjñānaṃ cittasahitaṃ devi śūnyālāyo bhavet || 120||

If, while having fixed the gaze on a material object, one were gently Dh. 96
to invert the gaze, [then] that cognizance [of the material object], connected with the thought [that is the focus of the inverted gaze], O Devi, would turn into the dissolution into the void.

The gaze has two components — the muscular and physiological fixation on the stimuli, and the mental fixation of the attention. Here, the first component should remain tuned into the material object, while the mental fixation of attention is drawn away from the mental representation of the object to where the mind is eager to go. The attention is spread over this pair, abandoning all other concerns, ideas, or associations. Then both components start to dissolve. Let them.

भक्त्युद्रेकाद्विरक्तस्य यादृशी जायते मतिः ।
सा शक्तिः शांकरी नित्यं भावयेत्तां ततः शिवः ॥ १२१ ॥

bhaktyudrekādviraktasya yādṛśī jāyate matiḥ |
sā śaktiḥ śāṃkarī nityaṃ bhāvayettāṃ tataḥ śivaḥ || 121||

Dh. 97 Whatever *mati*[74] is born of the aloofness resulting from an extreme devotion, it is made of the *parā-śakti* full of blissful tranquility. If one were to maintain that *mati*, then one would become *śiva.*

From time to time, excessive devotion results in an estrangement towards, or an aloof detachment from, the object of devotion. That feeling of estrangement might give rise to a mental gesture or expression that supports continuation of the detachment. That very mental gesture or expression carries the capacity to effect not only the detachment but also a blissful tranquility. If one were to maintain that gesture as dominant over all other thoughts, perceptions, desires, etc. for some time, then the state of *bhairava* would arise.

[74]Mental gesture.

वस्त्वन्तरे वेद्यमाने सर्ववस्तुषु शून्यता ।
तामेव मनसा ध्यात्वा विदितोऽपि प्रशाम्यति ॥ १२२॥

vastvantare vedyamāne sarvavastuṣu śūnyatā |
tāmeva manasā dhyātvā vidito'pi praśāmyati || 122||

"In the internal representation of an object there is no object whatsoever." Having mentally contemplated this emptiness, a learned man becomes tranquil. Dh. 98

Look at or listen to or touch something.

The impression created by this act of perception is subconsciously considered as the object perceived. Analyze the impression as having components like boundaries, contrasts, geometrical patterns, colors, overall size, etc. Realize that the location in space and dimension are results of a complex imputation that becomes evident, for example, when one slightly presses one eye with a finger so that the image becomes double, or crosses fingers to make tactile perception confused. Perceptual illusions in general make it apparent that the immediacy of perceptual imagery is an elaborate illusion. The "real" object of any perception is not given to the mind directly, but only indirectly. So, any thoughts, ideas, desires, aversions, etc. triggered by a perception are not about the "real" object, but about its mental "representation."

Contemplating ordinary, everyday experiences in this way, one becomes extremely introverted and calm. The state of *bhairava* is within reach.

किंचिज्ज्ञैर्या स्मृता शुद्धिः सा अशुद्धिः शम्भुदर्शने ।
न शुचिर्ह्यशुचिस्तस्मान्निर्विकल्पः सुखी भवेत् ॥ १२३॥

kiṃcijjñairyā smṛtā śuddhiḥ sā aśuddhiḥ śambhudarśane |
na śucirhyaśucistasmānnirvikalpaḥ sukhī bhavet || 123||

सर्वत्र भैरवोभावः सामान्येष्वपि गोचरः ।
नच तद्व्यतिरेकेण परोऽस्तीत्यद्वया गतिः ॥ १२४॥

sarvatra bhairavobhāvaḥ sāmānyeṣvapi gocaraḥ |
naca tadvyatirekeṇa paro'stītyadvayā gatiḥ || 124||

What is taught by those whose knowledge is sporadic as being purified is not purified at all, from the point of view of this philosophical system.[75] This is so, because, in comparison with the state of *bhairava*, nothing is more pure than it is impure, and nothing is more impure than it is pure. [Only when one is] devoid of polarizations [like pure/impure, etc.], might one be happy.

In every case, the perceptible by senses continuity between similar [things] is *bhairava*. Non-dual way [to explain the apparent variety of experiences in view of this all-pervasive nature of *bhairava* consists of the understanding that] "*That* does not exists without a contrast with *this*."

These two verses are not presenting a technique, but explicate some of the general principles behind practices of this tantra.

A contrast between "this" and "that" is just a dynamic of evolutes of *parā-śakti*. No matter how separate and distinct things seem to be, there is always a way to traverse from one to another without breaks in continuity, because "in the internal representation of an object there is no object whatsoever" (see verse 122). The division "that" and "this" is a superimposition, not an inherent difference.

[75] Called here "the doctrine of *śambhu*."

समः शत्रौ च मित्रे च समोमानावमानयोः ।
ब्रह्मणः परिपूर्णत्वादिति ज्ञात्वा सुखी भवेत् ॥ १२५॥

samaḥ śatrau ca mitre ca samomānāvamānayoḥ |
brahmaṇaḥ paripūrṇatvāditi jñātvā sukhī bhavet || 125||

Being impartial to an enemy and to a friend, impartial to expressions of honor or contempt, and thus having experienced [the state of *bhairava*] through being overflowed in every way with Brahman,[76] one might become happy. Dh.99

The major obstacles to the plasticity of psyche are emotional: aversions and longings. As Buddha says in Lokavipatti Sutta, the state of mind to aspire to is that when

> Desirable things[77] don't charm the mind,
> undesirable ones[78] bring no resistance.[79]

These four dimensions — material gain/loss, honor/disgrace, praise/censure, and physiological pleasure/pain — encompass many factors that, by acquiring the status of an imperative (like "strive for praise", "evade censure"), make "self" into puppet, a manipulated by strings, thus diminishing the bliss of self-will. Though by following such an imperative automatically, pleasure might be gained and pain avoided, there is no bliss in the pleasure and no peace in the absence of pain. One of the important points of the *Pratyabhijñā* system is that these "strings" are some of those expressions of one's own will that are devoid of awareness and self-reflection. Accurate recollection of those expressions of one's own will, that became such threads or chains, is the first step to reconfiguring them.

Here is an effective practice to become impartial. It lessens the "being driven by the waves of emotions, conditioned by memories." The practice has five steps:

1. Recollect and write down extreme cases of each of the four dimensions in as many personal details as possible.

[76] Infinite plasticity and all-pervasive spontaneity.
[77] Gain, status, praise, pleasure.
[78] Loss, disgrace, censure, pain.
[79] AN 8.6 Lokavipatti Sutta, translated by Thanissaro Bhikkhu

2. Recognize in everyday activities transitions (decisions, associations, arising of activity, cessation of activity) that are automatic (or almost automatic) and are motivated/energized by an affinity with items from step 1.[80]

3. Once a transition, and the items it has affinity with, are recognized, make the affinities as neutral as possible by two actions: by retracting the resolve to strive for or to evade situations associated with each of the items that the transition is motivated by; and then, by challenging the strength of the affinity. The challenge is accomplished by finding reasons why the strong affinity is not actually as good as was believed, or assumed, at the time of its formation,[81] and by finding how a more neutral affinity with the item is beneficial with respect to other personal values.

4. Having accomplished step 3 for the most pervasive transitions, return to the item on the list from step 1. If it is a positive item, retract the resolve to strive for the attainment (beyond what is required by reason). Or, if it is a negative item, resolve not to run from or resist it (beyond what is required by reason).

5. Form pairs of opposite items from step 1. Then, for each pair, perform the special *pūjā*, described below.

The *pūjā* is done in the following manner.[82] Bring both situations (making a pair of opposites) into attention focus, and try to become absorbed into both of them simultaneously. Successful absorption is marked by a sense of being in a great void. Then, find *mati* that is relatively stable in a neutral spot between both opposite situations. *Mati* should be stable despite shifting emphasis of moderate strength on one case vs. the other situation (the emphasis is created by varying concentration on one item, while still being absorbed into both). Maintain the *mati* active, while being absorbed into opposing situations, shifting emphasis between them for at least 10 minutes — to make the *mati* stable. In order to have

[80]An interruption of transition by means of meditative relaxation of effort is likely to bring the relevant item to the fore of attention.

[81]A significant reduction in level of awareness is almost always a strong reason for reducing strength of an affinity , if awareness is high on the scale of personal values.

[82]See verse 147.

a lasting effect, the *mati* should be guiding one's behavior outside this practice.

There is no need to make a single exhaustive list during step 1. Just a few items that seem related will suffice. As soon as one's awareness is expanded enough to allow the same treatment of new items, the practice can be repeated with a new list.

The are five major obstacles to overcome for making this practice useful:

a. becoming aware of the extreme cases and of the transitions which, by being almost automatic, are hard to detect;

b. maintaining attention on the cases and on the transitions long enough to perform analysis;

c. not being carried away by the emotional influence of the recollected situations;

d. becoming absorbed into both opposite cases simultaneously;

e. finding an adequate *mati* that is ethical and does not contradict major postulates and rules of the adopted philosophical system.

To deal with problem a., the systematic interruption and analysis of habitual actions, and meditation are helpful. To deal with problem b., concentration practices (*dhāraṇa* and *dhyāna*), or any activity requiring long chains of non-automatic mental operations, are recommended. To deal with problem c., one could cultivate the attitude of being just an observer. For problem d., start by calm breathing in and out with alternate concentration on corresponding "positive" and "negative" cases. At the same time, raise the level of attention on the "other" case until both levels of attention are about the same. To deal with problem e., a thorough knowledge of this philosophical system[83] and philosophy in general is of great help.
Bhagavad Gita has similar practice:

> Being impartial to an enemy and to a friend,
> impartial to expressions of honor or contempt,
> impartial to cold and hot, comfort and discomfort,
> one becomes becomes cleansed of attachments.[84]

[83] *Pratyabhijñā*

[84] *samaḥ śatrau ca mitre ca tathā mānāpamānayoḥ |*
śītoṣṇasukhaduḥkheṣu samaḥ saṅgavivarjitaḥ || BhG.12.18

न द्वेषम् भावयेत्क्वापि न रागं भावयेत्क्वचित् ।
रागद्वेषविनिर्मुक्तौ मध्ये ब्रह्म प्रसर्पति ॥ १२६ ॥

na dveṣam bhāvayetkvāpi na rāgaṃ bhāvayetkvacit |
rāgadveṣavinirmuktau madhye brahma prasarpati || 126||

Dh.100 If one were by no means and in no case to cultivate or encourage neither enmity nor affection, and when one becomes free from both affection and enmity, dwelling in-between [these two], one glides into the *Brahman.*[85]

Attachments and aversions, enmity and affections need constant affirmation. When affirmations are permanently absent, the attachments, aversions, affections, and enmities began to dissolve. This path is long and requires circumstances that will evoke personally significant attachments and aversions, but it might be useful if analytical ways suggested by the previous verse are not yet effective.

When experiencing pleasure, do not strive to prolong it; when recollecting the heights of ecstasy, do not strive to experience it again. When anticipating pain, contemplate the peak of that pain and mentally let it come, remembering what Marcus Aurelius said, "Nothing happens to anybody which he is not fitted by nature to bear. ... If you are distressed by anything external, the pain is not due to the thing itself but to your own estimate of it; and this you have the power to revoke at any moment."

[85]Infinite plasticity and all-pervasive spontaneity.

यदवेद्यं यदग्राह्यं यच्छून्यं यदभावगम् ।
तत्सर्वम् भैरवं भाव्यं तदन्ते बोधसम्भवः ॥ १२७॥

yadavedyaṃ yadagrāhyaṃ yacchūnyaṃ yadabhāvagam |
tatsarvam bhairavaṃ bhāvyaṃ tadante bodhasambhavaḥ || 127||

What cannot be understood, what cannot be grasped, what is empty, what is vanishing into nothingness — all these are about to transcend to [the state of] *bhairava*. When they do end up [transcending], then, simultaneously, pure awareness appears. Dh.101

Just observe when any of the listed conditions happens, be it something incomprehensible, or imperceptible, etc. It might trigger a transition to the state of *bhairava*, and the transition will be marked by emergence of pure awareness.

नित्ये निराश्रये शून्ये व्यापके कलनोज्झिते ।
बाह्याकाशे मनः कृत्वा निराकाशं समाविशेत् ॥ १२८ ॥

nityē nirāśraye śūnye vyāpake kalanojjhite |
bāhyākāśe manaḥ kṛtvā nirākāśaṃ samāviśet || 128||

Dh.102 If one were to place the *manas* into [something] continuous, or into [something] supportless, or into the void, or into [something] all-pervading, or into discontinued behavior [like the gap created by a sudden stop of an action], or into outer open space, then one might fall at once into the state of plenitude.

यत्र यत्र मनो याति तत्तत्तेनैव तत्क्षणम् ।
परित्यज्य अनवस्थित्या निस्तरङ्गस्ततो भवेत् ॥ १२९ ॥

yatra yatra mano yāti tattattenaiva tatkṣaṇam |
parityajya anavasthityā nistaraṅgastato bhavet || 129||

Towards whatever [thing, idea, object, feeling, etc.] the mind turns, Dh.103
having abandoned immediately that very thing, [idea, object, or feeling,] one might make it motionless through the lack of continual fixation.

Making the mind abandon whatever it turns to is done passively, by withdrawing attention from that thing and interrupting the chains of associations it evokes.

This is a description of "meditation without an object," as given by Swami Rama in "Meditation and Its Practice" [Ram98].

भया सर्वं रवयति सर्वदो व्यापकोऽखिले ।
इति भैरवशब्दस्य सन्ततोच्चारणाच्छिवः ॥ १३० ॥

bhayā sarvaṃ ravayati sarvado vyāpako'khile |
iti bhairavaśabdasya santatoccāraṇācchivaḥ || 130||

Dh.104 "With inherent luminosity, he roars up everything; he, all-bestowing, all-pervading, extending everywhere without gaps." From such continuous, uninterrupted utterance of the word *bhairava* [while having *mati*, that is expressing the functional qualities explained above, present,] one becomes *śiva*.

This alludes to an abbreviation of the phrase into the word *bhairava* which, being discovered by *nirvacana*[86] analysis, shows how the name expresses the nature of the deity.

In this verse, as explained by *Śivopādyāya*, the word *bhairava* is represented as a fusion of four syllables: *bhā-ai-ra-va*. *bhā* stands for luminosity; *ai* for the power of action; *ra* for *rava*, roaring, humming; *va* for *varuṇa*, all encompassing, all pervading space.

By continuously uttering *bhairava*, while internally bringing up the ideas behind the syllables — "With inherent luminosity, he roars up everything; he, all-bestowing, all-pervading, extending everywhere without gaps" — one can become immersed into contemplation of the same source of both sensory and verbal representations of the Universe, and this contemplation can lead to the state of *bhairava*.

There are at least a dozen interpretations of the word *bhairava*, broken into syllables as above — as presented in Tantraloka (TA.1.95-1.100) and in commentaries to *Vijñānabhairava*. Interested reader is referred to the Chapter 3 "Praxis: Saiva Kashmir" of [Kah98].

Note the trans-modal "with luminosity ... roars" and see verse 117.

---

[86]Traditional Indian semantic analysis of word meanings on the basis of syllables or even letters of that word.

अहं ममेदमित्यादि प्रतिपत्तिप्रसङ्गतः ।
निराधारे मनोयाति तद्ध्यानप्रेरणाच्छमी ॥ १३१ ॥

ahaṃ mamedamityādi pratipattiprasaṅgataḥ |
nirādhāre manoyāti taddhyānapreraṇācchamī || 131 ||

"I am; this is mine,..." Beginning thus, one leads *manas* towards a state devoid of any support, through excessive augmentation of the I-image. Dh.105

From the unfreezing of the static construct of "I," brought about by meditation [on the augmentations of many things regarded as "mine"], one becomes free of all emotions.

नित्यो विभुर्निराधारो व्यापकश्चाखिलाधिपः ।
शब्दान्प्रतिक्षणं ध्यायन्कृतार्थोऽर्थानुरूपतः ॥ १३२॥

nityo vibhurnirādhāro vyāpakaścākhiladhipaḥ |
śabdānpratikṣaṇaṃ dhyāyankṛtārtho'rthānurūpataḥ || *132*||

Dh.106 Continuous [in space and time], non-becoming, supportless, and all-pervading is the absolute sovereign [of my thoughts].

He who meditates every moment on these words, in conformity to their meaning, accomplishes the purpose [of this tantra — entering the state of *bhairava*].

This meditation is designed to make one's mind go from a place of observing the effects of the absolute sovereign's activity to merging with him. This transition has a marked change in the state of mind and happens abruptly. One of the signs of this transition is a good command of one's own thoughts. From this state, a transition to the state of *bhairava* can occur, if one avoids any speech, even internal.

अतत्त्वमिन्द्रजालाभम् इदं सर्वम् अवस्थितम् ।
किं तत्त्वमिन्द्रजालस्य इति दार्ढ्याच्छमं व्रजेत् ॥ १३३॥

atattvamindrajālābham idaṃ sarvam avasthitam |
kiṃ tattvamindrajālasya iti dārḍhyācchamaṃ vrajet || 133||

"It is established that this world has the appearance of a magic show and has no perceptible substance. What is the substance of an illusion?" Being firm [in asserting this], one might enter the state where there are no passions. Dh.107

आत्मनो निर्विकारस्य क्व ज्ञानं क्व च वा क्रिया ।
ज्ञानायत्ता बहिर्भावा अतः शून्यमिदं जगत् ॥ १३४ ॥

ātmano nirvikārasya kva jñānaṃ kva ca vā kriyā |
jñānāyattā bahirbhāvā ataḥ śūnyamidaṃ jagat || 134||

Dh.108 How can the "Immutable Self" perceive or be active? The ideas of things [perceived as] external [to self] depend upon [subjective] experiencing. Hence this world is empty [both internally and externally].

Thinking thus, one diminishes the urge and faculty to weave explanations not warranted by facts (see verse 138), and moves closer to the understanding of what in Buddhism is called *anatta* — the non-existence of inherent and immutable Ego.

The phrase "the world is empty" is to be understood as that there is nothing fixed, stable, or immutable that transcends both "external" and "internal." Therefore, a pursuit of such an "ultimate" thing is just chasing an illusion.

न मे बन्धो न मोक्षो मे भीतस्यैता विभीषिकाः ।
प्रतिबिम्बमिदं बुद्धेर्जलेष्विव विवस्वतः ॥ १३५॥

na me bandho na mokṣo me bhītasyaitā vibhīṣikāḥ |
pratibimbamidaṃ buddherjaleṣviva vivasvataḥ || 135||

[*Bhairava* says:] For me, there is no bondage of mundane existence nor is there for me liberation [from this bondage].

These two are just scarecrows for the fearful. This world is just a reflection of *buddhi*, diffusing light, as if it were a surface of water.

This not a technique, but a statement of philosophical principle: for the real Self, there is no bondage or liberation, but, rather, self-recognition in any complex configuration created by the interweaving of *tattva*-s. Lack of this recognition is the source of suffering. The recognition enables one to unwind from any complex configuration into the primordial state of *bhairava*.

इन्द्रियद्वारकं सर्वं सुखदुःखादिसंगमम् ।
इतीन्द्रियाणि संत्यज्य स्वस्थः स्वात्मनि वर्तते ॥ १३६ ॥

indriyadvārakaṃ sarvaṃ sukhaduḥkhādisaṃgamam |
itīndriyāṇi saṃtyajya svasthaḥ svātmani vartate || 136||

Dh.109 "Every organ of perception [presents] an uninterrupted series of contacts with pain, pleasure, etc."[87] Thus having [contemplated and therefore] abandoned the sensory streams, and being at ease, one abides in his true Self.

[87]Nuisance, soothing, distraction, attraction, etc.

ज्ञानप्रकाशकं सर्वं सर्वेणात्मा प्रकाशकः ।
एकमेकस्वभावत्वाज्ज्ञानं ज्ञेयं विभाव्यते ॥ १३७॥

jñānaprakāśakaṃ sarvaṃ sarveṇātmā prakāśakaḥ |
ekamekasvabhāvatvājjñānaṃ jñeyaṃ vibhāvyate || 137||

Everything is manifested through experience and through all things the Self is manifested. Experience and what is experienced are to be contemplated as one because of the single inherent nature of everything. Dh.110

The verses 138–153 explicate the philosophical background and general principles of the practices presented here.

मानसं चेतना शक्तिरात्मा चेतिचतुष्टयम् ।
यदा प्रिये परिक्षीणं तदा तद्भैरवं वपुः ॥ १३८ ॥

mānasaṃ cetanā śaktirātmā ceticatuṣṭayam |
yadā priye parikṣīṇaṃ tadā tadbhairavaṃ vapuḥ || 138||

When, O Dear, these four — mental disposition, understanding, the energy that mediates between the mental actions and physical actions, and the energies of breath — are diminished in all of their forms, then that is the *bhairava* state.

The state of bhairava occurs when none of the four categories of a stable mental dynamic dominate the psyche. Practices presented in this tantra deal with all four.

Here, the word "understanding" means the urge and the faculty to weave explanations not warranted by facts. This urge is the avoidance of the state of *epoche*, or the suspension of judgment.

निस्तरङ्गोपदेशानां शतमुक्तं समासतः ।
द्वादशाभ्यधिकं देवि यज्ज्ञात्वा ज्ञानविज्जनः ॥ १३९ ॥

nistaraṅgopadeśānāṃ śatamuktaṃ samāsataḥ |
dvādaśābhyadhikaṃ devi yajjñātvā jñānavijjanaḥ || 139 ||

A hundred prescriptions for stilling [those four] were formulated succinctly and augmented with twelve more, O Devi, having experienced which, [one becomes] a person of real knowledge.

अत्र चैकतमे युक्तो जायते भैरवः स्वयम् ।
वाचा करोति कर्माणि शापानुग्रहकारकः ॥ १४० ॥

atra caikatame yukto jāyate bhairavaḥ svayam |
vācā karoti karmāṇi śāpānugrahakārakaḥ || 140||

In these matters, engaged in [only a] single [practice out of 112] one becomes *bhairava* himself. He will be able to accomplish deeds by word alone, and he will be able to perform rites producing curses or conferring grace.

अजरामरतामेति सोऽणिमादिगुणान्वितः ।
योगिनीनां प्रियो देवि सर्वमेलापकाधिपः ॥ १४१ ॥
जीवन्नपि विमुक्तोऽसौ कुर्वन्नपि न लिप्यते ।

ajarāmaratāmeti so'ṇimādiguṇānvitaḥ |
yoginīnāṃ priyo devi sarvamelāpakādhipaḥ || 141||
jīvann api vimukto'sau kurvann api na lipyate |

He who is endowed with attributes like *aṇimā*, etc. approaches the state of being forever young and immortal. [He becomes] the dear of yoginis, O Devi, directing *melāpaka.* Though still living, [he is] liberated. Though performing that [that is, being the leader of *melāpaka*] [he is] not tainted by it.

Melāpaka is a ritual involving several yogis and yoginis, during which some taboos are broken. While violation of such taboos damages the spiritual development of an ordinary person, the adepts of this tantra remain unharmed.

श्री देव्युवाच ।

śrī devyuvāca |

Devī said:

इदं यदि वपुर्देव परायाश्च महेश्वर ॥ १४२॥
एवमुक्तव्यवस्थायां जप्यते को जपश्च कः ।
ध्यायते को महानाथ पूज्यते कश्च तृप्यति ॥ १४३॥
हूयते कस्य वा होमो यागः कस्य च किं कथम् ।

idaṃ yadi vapurdeva parāyāśca maheśvara || 142||
evamuktavyavasthāyāṃ japyate ko japaśca kaḥ |
dhyāyate ko mahānātha pūjyate kaśca tṛpyati || 143||
hūyate kasya vā homo yāgaḥ kasya ca kiṃ katham |

O *Deva*, if this is verily a form of *parā-śakti*, O *Maheśvara*, then, in the said condition, what is muttered during *japa* and what is *japa*?

What is being meditated upon, who is adored, and who becomes content?

To whom is the oblation offered and for whose benefit is the fire sacrifice performed, and how?

भैरव उवाच ।

bhairava uvāca |

Bhairava said:

एषात्र प्रक्रिया बाह्या स्थूलेष्वेव मृगेक्षणे ॥ १४४॥

eṣātra prakriyā bāhyā sthūleṣveva mṛgekṣaṇe || *144*||

Indeed, those are just external observances among the dense, O Gazelle-eyed!

भूयो भूयः परे भावे भावना भाव्यते हि या ।
जपः सोऽत्र स्वयं नादो मन्त्रात्मा जप्य ईदृशः ॥ १४५ ॥

bhūyo bhūyaḥ pare bhāve bhāvanā bhāvyate hi yā |
japaḥ so'tra svayaṃ nādo mantrātmā japya īdṛśaḥ || *145* ||

Ultimately, the cognition that is caused to arise in the state closest [to the state of *bhairava*] is *japa* in this system.

[If this cognition is a spontaneous humming sound, arising in the depth of one's being, then that] sound, being the very nature of *mantra*-s, is to be made into *japa* by continuous flow [into that state, closest to the state of *bhairava*].

By *japa* is usually understood a muttering of a particular *mantra*, like *Oṁ namaḥ śivāya*. This verse states that *japa*, in this *tantra*, is a continuous flow of attention, energy, awareness, etc. into a particular conception, cognition, percept, mental gesture, etc. that invokes the *parā* state of *śakti*. Whatever that might be is it is very individual. One of the more common cognitions is a continuous humming sound, originating in *suṣumnā*. This sound is not the ringing in the ears one can perceive sometimes. It is not evoked directly by some practice, but reveals itself when the mind is devoid of polarizations and *suṣumnā* is cleansed of impurities that block flows of *prāṇa* and *apāna.* When this sounds reveals itself, continuous awareness of it sound can become a gateway to the *parā* state of *śakti,* and thus to the state of *bhairava.*

ध्यानं हि निश्चला बुद्धिर्निराकारा निराश्रया ।
न तु ध्यानं शरीराक्षिमुखहस्तादिकल्पना ॥ १४६॥

dhyānaṃ hi niścalā buddhirnirākārā nirāśrayā |
na tu dhyānaṃ śarīrākṣimukhahastādikalpanā || 146||

The state of meditation is a continuous awareness, unwavering inspite of agitation, and having no refuge to which the mind can return. Meditation is not an arranging of body, eyes, head, hands etc. (that is, assuming a particular posture, making *mudrā*-s, performing *trāṭaka*, etc.).

पूजा नाम न पुष्पाद्यैर्या मतिः क्रियते दृढा ।
निर्विकल्पे महाव्योम्नि सा पूजा ह्यादराल्लयः ॥ १४७॥

pūjā nāma na puṣpādyairyā matiḥ kriyate dṛḍhā |
nirvikalpe mahāvyomni sā pūjā hyādarāllayaḥ || 147||

What is called *pūjā*[88] is not performed with flowers, [milk, ghee,] etc. That *mati* which is made stable in the vast expanse, devoid of *vikalpa*-s, that is the *pūjā*, for from adhering to it [comes] dissolution [of *manas*].

Dr.Roche adds in "The Radiance Sutras":

> Worship . . . means to let your heart pulse
> With the life of the universe
> Without thought and without reservation.

[88] A specialized worship.

अत्रैकतमयुक्तिस्थे योत्पद्येत दिनाद्दिनम् ।
भरिताकारता सात्र तृप्तिरत्यन्तपूर्णता ॥ १४८ ॥

atraikatamayuktisthe yotpadyeta dināddinam |
bharitākāratā sātra tṛptiratyantapūrṇatā || *148* ||

In this [tantra], when each day is devoted to performing [the same] single practice, she, in whose nature is the sense of satiety, then becomes the contentment and perpetual sense of fullness.

"She" here means *parā-śakti.* When *parā-śakti* is made predominant over *parā-aparā* and *aparā* forms regularly, then she reveals the state of *bhairava.*

महाशून्यालये वह्नौ भूताक्षविषयादिकम् ।
हूयते मनसा सार्धं स होमश्चेतनास्रुचा ॥ १४९ ॥

mahāśūnyālaye vahnau bhūtākṣaviṣayādikam |
hūyate manasā sārdhaṃ sa homaścetanāsrucā || *149* ||

The elements, the organs of perception, anything perceptible by the senses, etc. are all together mentally sacrificed into the fire that is dissolving into the great void. This is the fire sacrifice where consciousness is the wooden ladle.

Fire is a symbol of universal transmutability.

यागोऽत्र परमेशानि तुष्टिरानन्दलक्षणा ।
क्षपणात्सर्वपापानां त्राणात्सर्वस्य पार्वति ॥ १५० ॥

yāgo'tra parameśāni tuṣṭirānandalakṣaṇā |
kṣapaṇātsarvapāpānāṃ trāṇātsarvasya pārvati || 150||

The ritual here, O *Parameśānī*, is the contentment indicative of bliss, [coming] from him who destroys all ills, from him who protects all, O *Pārvatī*!

Contentment is an attribute of *parā-śakti*. See verse 148.

रुद्रशक्तिसमावेशस्तत्क्षेत्रं भावना परा ।
अन्यथा तस्य तत्त्वस्य का पूजा काश्च तृप्यति ॥ १५१ ॥

rudraśaktisamāveśastatkṣetraṃ bhāvanā parā |
anyathā tasya tattvasya kā pūjā kāśca tṛpyati || 151||

Total immersion into the *śakti* of *Rudra* — that is, "the field of merit" — is the ultimate realization. Otherwise, what ritual adoration of his essence [would there be], and who would be pleased?

The expression "field of merit" refers to the Buddhist notion from Anapanasati Sutta (Majjhima Nikaya 118).

स्वतन्त्रानन्दचिन्मात्रसारः स्वात्मा हि सर्वतः ।
आवेशनं तत्स्वरूपे स्वात्मनः स्नानमीरितम् ॥ १५२॥

svatantrānandacinmātrasāraḥ svātmā hi sarvataḥ |
āveśanaṃ tatsvarūpe svātmanaḥ snānamīritam || *152*||

In every aspect, one's own nature is just an extension of self-will, bliss, and pure awareness. Complete immersion [called the state of *turīya*] into the fundamental form of that nature is what is mentioned [in the Vedas] as bathing of the soul [in the sacred waters].

यैरेव पूज्यते द्रव्यैस्तर्प्यते वा परापरः ।
यश्चैव पूजकः सर्वः स एवैकः क्व पूजनम् ॥ १५३॥

yaireva pūjyate dravyaistarpyate vā parāparaḥ |
yaścaiva pūjakaḥ sarvaḥ sa evaikaḥ kva pūjanam || *153*||

Verily, *Śiva* alone is in whom the object of worship is, and he is every worshiper, high and low, whatever substances are used to honor or to please him.

This is a statement of ritual worship as an elaborate way of self-recognition.

व्रजेत्प्राणो विशेज्जीव इच्छया कुटिलाकृतिः ।
दीर्घात्मा सा महादेवी परक्षेत्रं परापरा ॥ १५४॥

अस्यामनुचरंस्तिष्ठन्महानन्दमयेऽध्वरे ।
तया देव्या समाविष्टः परं भैरवमाप्नुयात् ॥ १५५॥

vrajetprāṇo viśejjīva icchayā kuṭilākṛtiḥ |
dīrghātmā sā mahādevī parakṣetraṃ parāparā || *154* ||

asyāmanucaraṃstiṣṭhanmahānandamaye'dhvare |
tayā devyā samāviṣṭaḥ paraṃ bhairavamāpnuyāt || *155* ||

If, at one's own will, the breath is slow and in retrograde fashion, Dh.111
so that *prāṇa* is going out and *apāna* is going in, then she, the Great Devi in the *parā-aparā* state, [becomes] the ultimate place of pilgrimage.

Pursuing the depth of her and continuously performing the sacrifice, full of great happiness, [one becomes] possessed by her, by *śakti* [in *parā* state], and can reach the ultimate [state of] *bhairava*.

The "pursuit of the depth of her" means pursuit of the *parā-aparā* state of *śakti* that is transitioning into the *parā* state. "The sacrifice" here means the mental sacrifice mentioned in verse 149.

The technique of breathing in "retrograde fashion" is similar to that described in the verse 64. One has to direct flows of *prāṇa* and *apāna* with mental gestures and timing opposite to the natural cycle.

षट्शतानि दिवा रात्रौ सहस्राण्येकविंशतिः ।
जपो देव्याः समुद्दिष्टः सुलभो दुर्लभो जडैः ॥ १५६ ॥

ṣaṭśatāni divā rātrau sahasrāṇyekaviṃśatiḥ |
japo devyāḥ samuddiṣṭaḥ sulabho durlabho jaḍaiḥ || 156||

Dh.112 Twenty one thousand, six hundred times every day and night the *japa*[89] of *Devī* is clearly articulated (by sounds of breathing). [It is] easy to acquire [as a mantra], [but] for those who are not intelligent — difficult.

"Twenty one thousand, six hundred times" means every breath of a day and a night. This number is obtained if every breath takes four seconds. The number of breaths per twenty four hours is individual and might be quite different from the number given.

What does it mean "to acquire as a mantra"? It means that the barely felt sound of unobstructed breath is allowed to be in the center of both hearing and production of speech.

This verse is the last in the technical part of the text.

[89]See verse 145.

The following verses are quite traditional instructions on the transmission of this *tantra.*

इत्येतत्कथितं देवि परमामृतमुत्तमम् ।
एतच्चनैव कस्यापि प्रकाश्यं तु कदा चन ॥ १५७॥
परशिष्ये खले क्रूरे अभक्ते गुरुपादयोः ।
निर्विकल्पमतीनां तु वीराणामुन्नतात्मनाम् ॥ १५८॥
भक्तानां गुरुवर्गस्य दातव्यं निर्विशण्कया ।
ग्रामो राज्यं पुरं देशः पुत्रदारकुटुम्बकम् ॥ १५९॥
सर्वमेतत्परित्यज्य ग्राह्यमेतन्मृगेक्षणे ।
किमेभिरस्थिरैर्देवि स्थिरं परमिदं धनम् ।
प्राणा अपि प्रदातव्या न देयं परमामृतम् ॥ १६०॥

ityetatkathitaṃ devi paramāmṛtamuttamam |
etaccanaiva kasyāpi prakāśyaṃ tu kadā cana || *157*||
paraśiṣye khale krūre abhakte gurupādayoḥ |
nirvikalpamatīnāṃ tu vīrāṇāmunnatātmanām || *158*||
bhaktānāṃ guruvargasya dātavyaṃ nirviśaṇkayā |
grāmo rājyaṃ puraṃ deśaḥ putradārakuṭumbakam || *159*||
sarvametatparityajya grāhyametanmṛgekṣaṇe |
kimebhirasthirairdevi sthiraṃ paramidaṃ dhanam |
prāṇā api pradātavyā na deyaṃ paramāmṛtam || *160*||

Thus, the excellent *Paramāmṛta* is retold, O *Devī.* This [teaching] should never be revealed to just anyone: [not] to a pupil of another, [not] to a mischievous or cruel, not to irreverent towards guru's feet.

But to those who are vigourous and honest in their intentions, to those who are intent on attaining the non-polarization as their guiding principle, to those who are devoted to the family of gurus, it is to be communicated without hesitation.

Village, realm, city, country, son, wife, household — all this having been abandoned, this [tantra] is to be embraced.

For how, O Gazel-eyed, by those who are full of doubts and lack practical knowledge, can this tantra be transmitted without distortions?

Even if threatened with death, one should not reveal this teaching of the *Paramāmṛta.*

The advice to abandon village, realm, city, country, son, wife and household in order to practise this tantra is to be understood within the context of medieval India, where it was originally given, and not to be taken literally nowadays. There is simply no need. Still, expect to become at odds with village, realm, etc. as a result of practicing it.

श्री देव्युवाच ।

śrī devyuvāca |

Devī said:

देवदेव माहदेव परितृप्तास्मि शंकर ॥ १६१॥
रुद्रयामलतन्त्रस्य सारमद्यावधारितम् ।
सर्वशक्तिप्रभेदानां हृदयं ज्ञातमद्य च ॥ १६२॥
इत्युक्त्वानन्दिता देवी कण्ठे लग्ना शिवस्य तु ॥ १६३॥

devadeva māhadeva paritṛptāsmi śaṃkara || 161||
rudrayāmalatantrasya sāramadyāvadhāritam |
sarvaśaktiprabhedānāṃ hṛdayaṃ jñātamadya ca || 162||
ityuktvānanditā devī kaṇṭhe lagnā śivasya tu || 163||

O *Deva*, O great *Deva*, I am completely satisfied, O beneficent one!

The essence of *Rudrayāmala* tantra is now ascertained, and the source of the variety of *śakti*-s is understood. Having spoken thus, delighted *Devī* merged back into *Śiva*'s throat.

Concepts

All concepts and technical terms in here are interpreted from the positions of the *Pratyabhijñā* system of philosophy (see [Sem08], [Tor02] and [Sin03a]).

There are two basic concepts: *śiva* and *śakti*. *Śakti* is a dynamic aspect of *śiva*. *Śiva* is hypokeimenon of all manifestation, and he has a multitude of states or forms.[90] There is nothing in the Universe, as it is reflected in the mind, that is not *śiva*; in the same way there is nothing in nature that is not a form of energy.

Of the many states of *śiva*, there is a special, distinguished state that is called *bhairava*. It is undifferentiated, unvaried condition, or form, that lacks any particulars, but is full of all potentialities. The state of *bhairava* is like the stillness and tranquility of homogeneous air. One of the inherent characteristics of air is the presence of ever appearing and dissolving fluctuations of pressure, temperature and density. Similarly, there is the primordial, ever present throbbing of fluctuations in *śiva*. This throbbing is called *spanda*.

When fluctuations of pressure occur in still air, they might dissipate without any manifested phenomena, or they might give birth to wind or whirls. In the same way, *spanda* might give rise to a more differentiated state of *śiva*. The energy of fluctuations in the state of *bhairava* is called *bhairavī*, or *parāśakti*, or ultimate potentiality.

When this energy of pressure fluctuations transforms into wind or whirls, the air becomes manifestly non-uniform, or differentiated. This differentiation might become sounds, lenses causing visual distortions, twisters, etc. Similarly, *parāśakti* might give rise to specific potentialities, or energies, that cause sensory perception, speech, thoughts, emotions, etc.

A specific form of the *parāśakti* can be either of the *parā-aparā* type or of the *aparā* type, and is called N-*śakti*.[91]

[90] *vapus*, *rūpa*.

[91] Here N denotes a particular experience or manifestation or process.

The *parā-aparā* type of *śakti* is the potentiality that is born of differentiations caused by *parāśakti*. *Parā-aparā* can directly dissolve into *parāśakti*. The differentiations caused by it may dissolve or evolve into a self-perpetuating cycle of arising, relative stability, and cessation. In the last case *parā-aparā-śakti* becomes a multitude of *aparā-śakti*-s.

The *aparā* type of *śakti* is the potentiality that is born of differentiations caused by *parā-aparāśakti*. Like turbulence in the air, in which the disappearance of one whirl causes new disturbances in the flow of air, so are differentiations and manifestations that are born of the *aparā* type of *śakti*. Cessation of one phenomena gives birth to others. The perpetuation of arising, relative stability, and cessation of phenomena is called *saṃsāra*. Abiding in the state of *bhairava* is the cessation of *saṃsāra*, or *nirvana*.

The state of *bhairava* in which the energy of fluctuations is at the threshold of causing some phenomena is called *prabhu*.

Below is a vocabulary of concepts required for understanding the philosophy and some of the practices of the *Pratyabhijñā* system of Kashmir Shaivism. Many terms in this vocabulary occur in other philosophical systems of India, and their meanings can be quite different, at times, from system to system. Only the meanings used in the *Pratyabhijñā* system are pointed at here.

It should be noted that the most basic concepts are left undefined, for they are not reducible to other concepts (in the same way the concepts of a dot, a line, and a plane are left undefined in Euclidean geometry). However, since it might be easier to form in the mind the correct ideas behind words with the help of approximations, I've attempted to formulate such approximations based on my own experiences. All such approximations are made on the experiential plane of meaning; that is, in order to provide for practical applications.

In some cases, a definition is given by means of several expressions separated by semicolons. The reader should try to form a concept that is "in the middle" of all those expressions.

The order of terms is non-alphabetical, but is organized in such a way that any definition refers, in most cases, only to definitions prior to it.

prakāśa is that which manifests itself in every mental phenomena;
energy that is the carrier of all stimulation,[92] whether

[92] "Stimulation" is understood here as any immediate cause of activation

because of sensory input, memory, or imagination;
substratum of all sense-datum;
that which always (at all times and in all cases) illuminates.[93]

The concept of *prakāśa* is central for the formulation of many concepts of Trika: Tantraloka even gives the condition for liberation, quoting Yogacara, as "liberation comes from illumination of everything."[94]

This illumination is inherent in one's being. As Buddha said,[95] "Luminous is the mind."

vimarśa — shifting, non-uniform self-reflection, that is alternating between various degrees of affection and detachment.

svātantrya — the freedom of will;
self-will.

svātantrya is a quality of *vimarśa*. From the perspective of action, it is defined as "the principal authorship and the supremacy to be such."[96]

camatkāra — the aesthetic experience of the bliss of *svātantrya*.

cit — the Absolute, which is the substratum of all manifestation;
a pure perceptive attention that has two aspects — *prakāśa* and *vimarśa*.

It is also called *parāsaṃvid*, or the ultimate *saṃvid*.

Through *vimarśa*, *cit* possesses the absolute free will (*svātantrya*) and, therefore, *camatkāra*.

śiva — *cit*, when the *vimarśa* aspect is emphasized;
the Absolute that spontaneously, like an infinitesimal pulsation, by the power of free will, emanates the Universe as a self-reflection.

---

of mental things; light falling onto light receptors in the eye, the energy of concentration that allows one to imagine non-existing things, the power of association that brings memories to mind — all these are examples of stimulation. It should be noted that stimulation might be below the threshold of perception.

[93] *prakāśonāma yaścāyaṃsarvatraiva prakāśate* TA.1.54.a

[94] *uktaṃ ca śrīyogācāre mokṣaḥ sarvaprakāśanāt* TA.6.58.b

[95] Pabhassara Sutta, AN 1.49

[96] Comment to the *sūtra* 20 of *Pratyabhijñāhṛdayam svātantryam atha kartṛtvaṃ mukhyam īśvaratāpi ca*

On a personal level, "being like *śiva*" means to be in the state of benevolent, happy tranquility, possessing unlimited creativity as the potentiality.

śakti unmodified by context, pure form of potentiality; unmodified by context, pure form of transition; infinitely elastic wave of energy.

Various forms of *śakti* are projections of the basic form — that of "the spontaneous aspiration" of *śiva* to manifest the entire Universe.

There are many forms, or projections, of *śakti*. All of them are qualities of *śiva*. The most fundamental for the *Pratyabhijñā* system are *icchāśakti*, *jñanaśakti*, *kriyāśakti*, and *māyāśakti*.

cicchakti the ability to illuminate, to attend to.[97]

ānandaśakti the ability to experience bliss; *śiva*'s freedom of will.[98]

icchāśakti astonishment, surprise at the one's own freedom of will.[99]

Gaining freedom is manifested through astonishment. Flight from freedom is the flight towards the certain, controllable, and predictable.

jñānaśakti the ability to have direct experience (lit. to touch).[100]

kriyāśakti the ability to be related or connected in any way.[101]

tattva an attribute, a quality of mental "things" (ideas, percepts, gestalts, volitions, emotions, feelings, actions, speech, and anything that might be an object of introspection);
that which patterns fragmentation, breaks the whole into parts, but by doing so, provides for comparability between distinct entities, or particulars (*svalakṣana*-s);
type of dynamic in *prakāśa*.

[97] ...*prakāśarūpatā cicchaktiḥ* AbhTs.1.5
[98] ...*tasya ca svātantryamānandaśaktiḥ* AbhTs.1.5
[99] ...*taccamatkāra icchāśaktiḥ*... AbhTs.1.5
[100] ...*āmarśātmakatā jñānaśaktiḥ*... AbhTs.1.5
[101] *sarvākārayogitvaṃ kriyāśaktiḥ* AbhTs.1.5

A *tattva* may be compounded with several other *tattva*-s; it might have another *tattva* as a component; and it might be perceptible under some circumstances.

An important aspect of all *tattva*-s, other than *śiva-tattva*, is that there are three modes of expression:

being absent;

being present to some degree, but amenable to vanishing or dissolving;

being present to some degree, but rigidly split away from vanishing.

The practical goal of the *Pratyabhijñā* system is the reconfiguration of mental processes that get rid of those *tattva* expressions that are rigidly split from vanishing. The practices described in *Vijñānabhairava* tantra help with such reconfiguration.

According to Trika, there are 36 fundamental *tattva*-s:

śiva-tattva

śakti-tattva

sadāśiva-tattva

īśvara-tattva

śuddhavidyā-tattva

māyā-tattva

kalā-tattva

vidyā-tattva

rāga-tattva

kāla-tattva

niyati-tattva

puruṣa-tattva

prakṛti-tattva

buddhi-tattva

ahaṃkāra-tattva

manas-tattva

five *karmendriya*-s

five *jñānedriya*-s

five *tanmātra*-s

five *mahābhūta*-s.

A detailed discussion of all *tattva*-s can be found in [Sem08].

Each *tattva* is sustained and supported by the *tattva*-s above it. The topmost, *śiva-tattva*, is therefore called *anāśrita*, that is, "not supported."

Various degrees of their expression cause the multitude of personal experiences and states of mind. Analysis of experiences and states using *tattva*-s as dimensions, or categories, is integral to the path of the *Pratyabhijñā* system.

Although there is a strong similarity between the lowest 25 *tattva*-s and the *tattva*-s of the *Saṃkhya* system, there is no equivalency between them.

vāyu a subtle energy;
a dynamic of activation of specific neurotransmitters in various parts of the nervous system;
a wave of expression of specific neurotransmitters.

According to *Śivasvarodaya*,[102] there are 10 types of subtle energies: *prāṇa*, *apāna*, *samāna*, *udāna*, *vyāna*, *nāga*, *kūrma*, *kṛkala*, *devadatta*, *dhanañjaya*.

prāṇa is predominant at the moment the breathing in starts;
apāna is predominant at the moment the breathing out starts;
samāna — in the process of digestion;
udāna — in energy surge through *suṣumnā* when *prāṇa* and *apāna* are in equilibrium;
vyāna — in the state of *samādhi*. It is felt as pervading everything. It makes maintaining *āsana* and other functions of the body effortless during hours of remaining in *samādhi*.

nāga manifests itself during vomiting;
kūrma — in blinking of eyes;
kṛkala — in sneezing;
devadatta — in yawning;
dhanañjaya keeps integrity of the physical body after

[102] ShSv.42-47

death (and is, probably, the source of the notion "zombie").

A *vāyu* might be perceived as "inner flow" or "touch" or "cloud of sensation" in some parts of the body, especially when the flow is interrupted or obstructed. Sensations might differ from person to person, but what is important is that flows of the vital energies might be perceived and even controlled. *Prāṇāyāma* is a set of practices that accomplishes just such control. For practical guidance on *prāṇāyāma*, see [SR98] and [Iye99].

prāṇa — the *vāyu*, or subtle energy, that is predominant at the moment the breathing in starts.

It facilitates mental agitation and serves as "energetic background" for many processes. *Prāṇa* originates in *kanda* (a spot inside the body about five thumb-widths below the navel)[103] and is transmuted into other *vāyu*-s. The importance of the control of *prāṇa* for a philosophical inquiry and for any yogic practice comes from the close connection between psychological processes and flows of *prāṇa*, and between *prāṇa* and physiological processes. Control over *prāṇa* is a prerequisite for control over mind. Strong disequilibrium in *prāṇa* distribution is a source of errors in reasoning, especially in operations on ill-defined concepts.

apāna — the *vāyu*, or subtle energy, that is predominant at the moment the breathing out starts.

nāḍī — channel along which *vāyu*-s flow. It is not necessarily a physical channel like a nerve or a vein, but a persistent pattern of neurotransmitter expression. These patterns are called "channels" because they are felt that way. According to tantric scriptures, there are many thousands of *nāḍī*-s throughout the body. Of them, three are the most important for any yogic practice: *iḍā*, *piṅgalā*, and *suṣumnā*.

cakra — an intersection of three or more *nāḍī*-s. When flows of subtle energies are obstructed, *cakra* might be felt as a spot about one thumb-width in size. The "petals" of a

[103] *prāṇaḥ kandāt prabhṛtyeva tathāpyatra na susphuṭaḥ* TA.6.49

cakra are experienced as sensations of directional flows to/from the central spot of the *cakra*. Different numbers of *cakra*-s are recognized by different traditions, but six *cakra*-s are recognized universally. See Appendix for a map of *cakra*-s. For further details on *nāḍī*-s, *cakra*-s, "petals," etc. see [SR98].

vikalpa a state of polarization that makes anything manifested to be defined on an X/not-X scale;
antithesis of opposites.

In the emotional sphere *vikalpa* of X is born of deprivation, resulting from the lack of expedients to satisfy a particular desire X. Such *vikalpa* is made stable by the resolve to satisfy X. The resolve is born of the inherent-in-one's-self free will.[104]

Vikalpa is in opposition to recognizing the primordial unity of one's own self. It is an obstacle to *yoga*.[105]

In the sphere of perception/cognition: *vikalpa* is an ascertainment casting duality.[106] *Vikalpa* is that which, having inhibited the fact of the selectivity of attention by means of *māyā*, projects itself as the disjunction between what is manifested and the unmanifested counterpart of the manifested.[107]

It projects duality onto the body, onto vital energies (*vāyu*-s), onto perception and imagination, making everything appear as if in a cloud — perspective is very limited, but nothing restricting it can be seen — expressing *vimarśa* through a contrast between what it makes into opposites by manifesting one and rejecting the other. *vikalpa* is an expression of "I am" through contrasts.

In the sphere of activity *vikalpa*-s manifest themselves as the synchronous contraction/relaxation of compli-

[104] *vikalpaḥ kasyacit svātmasvātantryād eva susthiraḥ* |
upāyāntarasāpekṣyaviyogenaiva jāyate || TA.5.3

[105] *kasyacittu vikalpo'sau svātmasaṃskaraṇaṃ prati* TA.5.4.a

[106] *nāsau vikalpaḥ sa hyukto dvayākṣepī viniścayaḥ* K1.6.1.cd

[107] *cittattvaṃ māyayā hitvā bhinna evāvabhāti yaḥ*
dehe buddhāvatha prāṇe kalpite nabhasīva vā
pramātṛtvenāhamiti vimarśo'nyavyapohanāt
vikalpa eva sa parapratiyogyavabhāsajaḥ K1.6.4-5

mentary muscle groups,[108] as tides of breathing in and out, when waning of *prāṇa* is synchronized with waxing of *apāna*.

It is through using *vikalpa*-s that personal likes/dislikes, emotions, and affective states of mind pervade all of the Universe, as reflected in one's being. As soon as there is indefiniteness, it becomes amalgamated with various likes/dislikes. In the course of practicing detachment and dispassion,[109] which is an essential component of any systematic practice, this amalgamation disappears, uncovering the indefiniteness of experience and of being as such.

karma — lasting aftereffects of an action, physical or mental (especially of an intent), that disturbs equilibrium of some configuration either in the cognitive or in the emotional spheres, or in the sphere of activity.

The best action is that which leaves no traces, that is, it is *karma*-free, for *karma* is created by acting or intending to act beyond what is required by the situation.

Karma is neither absolute determinism, nor the will of God, nor a random conglomeration of circumstances.[110] If you throw a pebble above your head and it falls down and hits you, this is not the law of karma at work, but laws of physics.

How strong the after-effects are, and what the practical consequences of their existence will be, is not deterministic. Rather, it depends on many other things, particularly, on how spiritually advanced one is.[111] Whether *karma* is deemed positive or negative depends on whether it reduces or strengthens *vikalpa*-s.

Karma has the potential to cause physical illness: an intention, even if not yet expressed, might cause lasting changes in flows of *prāṇa*, *apāna*, etc.; lasting changes in

---

[108] If the biceps are contracted, the triceps are automatically relaxed.

[109] *Vairagya*, as understood in the Yoga Sutra. It is a complete understanding of how the world, observed directly or known through literary tradition, subjugates one's will, with the condition that such understanding is born of a reduction in the thirst for desirable things. *dṛṣṭānuśravikaviṣayavitṛṣṇasyavaśīkārasaṃjñāvairāgyam* YS.I.15

[110] Tittha Sutta AN.III.61

[111] Lonaphala Sutta AN.III.99, Sivaka Sutta SN.XXXVI.21

such flows cause, with time, physiological disfunctions, and those might lead to an illness.

kalā elemental skills;
micro-skills.

māyā the lack of clear perception of the presence of the *tattva*-s, starting with *kalā* and ending with *pṛthvī*;[112] whatever is possessing of resistance, opposition to transitions — that is an expression of *māyā*.[113]

Māyā avoids being manifested by constant incitement of habitual, impulsive, or automatized actions. The incitement is caused by selective masking of conditions that determine the relevancy of their activation, thus leaving dominant only desire/action aspects. Because of the consequences of this incitement *māyā* is called bewildering.[114]

The following five *tattva*-s, beginning with *kalā-tattva* and ending with *niyati-tattva*, are collectively referred to as *kañcuka*-s (or "armors of an individual"). Their common property is to strengthen with time and to become more and more rigid.

kalā-tattva transfer of the energy of will onto the field of habitual, impulsive, or automatized actions;
automatism of action, skill.

The presence of *kalā-tattva* provides for virtuoso performance in all arts, but because of the automatism, it limits to some degree the creativity of the performer. It also provides for obsessive and impulsive behaviors, like playing video-games or Internet browsing.

The power of *kalā-tattva* to shape consciousness is so strong and universal among humans that it is said by *Bṛhaspati* (quoted in TA.9.208b) to be like a second *citi*. Consciousness shaped only by *śiva-tattva*, *śakti-tattva*, *sadāśiva-tattva*, *īśvara-tattva*, and *śuddhavidyā-tattva* has no definite form; it is like the Heraclitean river, which stays the same despite the flows of water

---

[112] *kalādīnāṃ tattvānām avivekomāyā* SS.III.3
[113] *bhāvānāṃ yatpratīghāti vapur māyātmakaṃ hi tat* TA 3.10.a
[114] *māyā vimohinī nāma kalāyāḥ kalanaṃ sthitam* VBh.95.a

being never the same. *Kalā-tattva* changes that indefiniteness — as if adding polished facets to a natural ruby.

The impulse or the incitement behind the *kalā-tattva* is *māyā*. This is so, because in the inner world only consistent and automatic concealment is effective. *Karma* expresses itself through *kalā-tattva* (but not only through it).

vidyā-tattva transfer of the energy of will onto the field of meanings, abstractions, and scripts of actions;
that which marks what is pleasurable, what is suffering, and what is neither, separately and in addition to the instinct; that which relates any knowledge to the needs of the corporeal body and of the material existence; *pramātṛ* of stimulation coming from the corporeal body (that is, from internal organs, from muscles, from joints); that which integrates proprioceptive signals into perception.

In general, *vidyā-tattva* operates on meta-levels, being an instrument of actions upon *buddhi*; that is, it is not being augmented onto *grāhya* directly.[115] *Vidyā-tattva* primes perception, action, or desire to conform to general categories.

For example, a percept of fire augmented with *vidyā-tattva* might acquire qualities like "warmth" or "burning," even if the subject of perception is too far from the fire to feel either warmth or burning. Another example is given by composing a sentence to comply with a particular grammatical structure, grammar being a meta-level of ordinary language.

Though quite limited in purpose, *vidyā-tattva*, being a realization of *vidyāśakti*, facilitates counteracting *māyā*.[116]

rāga-tattva transfer of the energy of will into nurturing an attachment;
an attribute that provides for a subtle restoration of desire (potentially directed towards a new object) even

---

[115] *tattvaṃ vidyākhyamasṛjatkaraṇaṃ paramātnamaḥ MrA*

[116] *tasyaiśvaryasvabhāvasya paśubhāve prakāśikā* |
vidyāśaktiḥ tirodhānakarī māyābhidhā punaḥ || IPK.3.1.7

after the desire was completely satisfied;[117] intense affection that is not specific, that is without a definite object.[118]

Rāga-tattva prevents positive or negative emotions from becoming just memories. It is more like a resolve to keep these emotions relevant to one's self.

Whether some experience would be positive or negative from the point of view of feelings depends in part on physiology. But whether *rāga-tattva* is attached to the experience or not is more a result of one's own intentions.

Sometimes one can observe how *rāga-tattva* is affixed to some positive or negative experiences when the experiences are recollected. This augmentation might be accompanied by thoughts like "I will pursue this," or "I really like that," or "This is important for me," etc.

Whatever inner construct was created with intention, the support for its existence might by removed by unintending. After the support is removed, the flux of things will gradually dissolve it.

kāla-tattva in the domain of perception and knowledge, it is an attribute of duration, the quality of having a location in time, the mark of being "before/after" some event;
in the domain of actions, sense of pace (that which enables one to sing in sync with music or to mirror synchronously the actions of another);
in the domain of desires, it is the duration of postponement of gratification beyond which a lack of satisfaction causes distress, anxiety, etc., or the timing of some events (like when one resolves "I will wake up at exactly at 7:40 a.m." and does wake up at that time).

niyati-tattva strong inclination towards a particular way of acting, thinking, or feeling;
kalā, devoid of the strength of immediacy;
transition between apparent cause and apparent effect

---

[117] *rāgatattvamiti proktaṃ yattatraivoparañjakam* |
na cāvairāgyamātraṃ tattatrāpy āsaktivṛttitaḥ || TA.9.200
viraktāv api tṛptasya sūkṣmarāgavyavasthiteḥ | TA.9.201a

[118] *rāgo'bhiṣvaṅgātmā viṣayacchedaṃ vinaiva sāmānyaḥ* TP.48.ab

(*niyati-tattva* is the link between *karma* and the consequences of it);
in the domain of perception and knowledge, it is the bias of a syllogism, especially of logical fallacies;
in the domain of actions, it is a habitual coordination of muscular activity (for example, stepping on an unmoving escalator, that was moving in the past, creates muscular activation inadequate to the situation);
in the domain of desires/will, it is the absoluteness of acceptance/rejection (like "this is intolerable," "that is the best thing ever," "I never can do that," etc.).

Whatever is possessing *niyati-tattva* acquires an appearance of "necessity."

kañcuka an armor of an individual;
one the five *tattva*-s: *kalā-tattva*, *vidyā-tattva*, *rāga-tattva*, *kāla-tattva*, and *niyati-tattva*.

The presence of *kañcuka*-s is revealed by the following persistent and pervasive phenomena:

preservation of "I" is a habit; that is, a set of skills invoked almost instinctively, personal speech being the primary example;

knowledge is dedicated to survival, either personal or of some substitute (like family, tribe, social group, philosophical system, scientific theory, etc.); the validity of knowledge is derived from authority; asking for opinions of an authority is the origin of knowledge;

relishing the very desire for "I" to be;

a resolve that an absence of "I" expression should last no longer than some preset period of time (that might vary with circumstances);

the conviction that it is *necessary* for "I" to be.

There might be other expressions. Any aspect of one's individuality might have several armors.

A very important practice with regard to the *kañcuka*-s is deconstruction of long-term, persistent expressions of them in one's own behavior. By conscious removal of actual expressions of these five *tattva*-s, an "individual," devoid of armors, would be eventually dissolved by the flux of things.

The point of the practice is not to get killed, or to die from exposure, or to become a mindless cult follower of some strong willed individual or group, but to get rid of irrational rigidity and to understand how the armors and the very idea of an unchangeable and sharply bounded "individual" contribute to self-perpetuating unhappiness, stress, and pain.

mahābhūta-s these represent types of ideas, or patterns of dividing stream of stimulation into entities:
pṛthivī (earth) type indicates an idea of something fixed, like a solid body — not subject to change due to the context, neither in substance nor in form;
jala (water) type indicates an idea of something like a fluid, of something that has an invariant substance, but a form completely dependent on the environment;
tejas (fire) type indicates an idea of something like the light, of intensity, energy, an idea of something having no definite form, but adopting attributes of the environment;
vāyu (air) indicates an idea of something like air, all-pervading; of something having no manifested substance or form, but the presence of which is inferred from manifested elements;
ākāśa (ether) indicates an idea that stands for absence of something else, an idea of the void.

All of these types can be illustrated with a favorite object of Indian philosophical discourse — a jar. The jar as a solid body is an example of *pṛthivī*. The water in the jar is an example of *jala*. The round and hollow shape of the jar is conveyed by light gradients, which exemplify *tejas*. The usability of the jar for cooking, not just for holding water, is an example of *vāyu*. And an abstraction of a jar, as a rigid shape devoid of space and time particularizations — the empty space within — is an example of *ākāśa*.

Another illustration of *mahābhūta*-s is afforded by a Japanese garden: *pṛthivī* are the stones, *jala* is the flow of water shaped by the stones; *tejas* is the light that integrates elements of the garden into a landscape; *vāyu* is *fuzei*, or that breeze of feelings evoked by the experience of being in the garden, which cannot easily be attributed to any particular component; *ākāśa* is the contrasting void left after exiting the garden, when the enchantment of *fuzei* is dispersed by the flood of city irritants.

One of the important applications of the concept of *mahābhūta*-s to the analysis of psychological processes is the analysis of ideas of "self." Ego attempts to present the "self" as an unchangeable, sharply bounded entity — by projecting *pṛthivī* attribute onto it. The *pṛthivī-tattva*, being the last in the sequence of *tattva*-s, partakes in and is supported by all *tattva*-s. Thus, is it pervasive, robust, and very difficult to dissolve. The weakening of *pṛthivī-tattva*, that affords local dissolution of it in every context, is called in Buddhism "stream-entry."

If that attempt of Ego fails, the next presentation is using *jala* as the pattern, etc. In reality, in different contexts, the "self" might have different patterns. One of the fundamental ideas of Buddha is that of *anātman* — all of these patterns are projected onto "self" and are not inherent in it.

sattva luminosity, differentiating real from unreal;
source of attachment to happiness and knowledge.[119]

rajas transience;[120]
source of passion and attachment to action.[121]

tamas inertia, resistance to change;
source of attachment to delusions.[122]

guṇa a pervasive attribute, one of the three: *sattva*, *rajas*, or *tamas*.[123]

[119] *sattvaṃ sukhe sañjayati...* BhG XIV.9.a
[120] *... rajaḥ karmaṇi bhārata* BhG XIV.9.a
[121] *rajo rāgātmakaṃ viddhi tṛṣṇāsāṅgasamudbhavam* BhG XIV.7.a
[122] *jñānamāvṛtya tu tamaḥ pramāde sañjayatyuta* BhG XIV.9.b
[123] *sattvaṃ rajastama iti guṇāḥ prakṛtisambhavāḥ* BhG XIV.5.a

manas — the "inner eye" that coordinates sensory inputs from different modalities and from the memory to ensure coherent experience;
the faculty of introspection that enables one to see arising and fading of ideas or images in one's mind;
the organ of perception that allows one to become aware of inner states, like sadness, joy, desire, aversion, etc.;
a stable area that is the hub of the mind's activity, and that provides a general framework for resolving indeterminacy and defines the general direction of activity.

buddhi — the cognitive faculty of forming, applying, and manipulating knowledge;
the faculty of reasoning and establishing certainty.

The Bhagavad Gita states the importance of *buddhi* in this way: "what is defined as happiness beyond any limit is beyond perception, and is to be grasped by *buddhi*."[124]

Buddhi deals with concepts that are knowledge, not notions. Notions are constructs of *manas* and are merely loose associations of several mental constructs.

There is a very important difference between concepts that are knowledge and those that are notions. Definiteness of notions is derived from perceptual similarity (expressed by "It seems that way"), while that of knowledge is from procedural measurement, based on the most sharp of perceptual distinctions, (expressed by "The measure is such").

A notion is quite easily morphed by strong emotions, because judgments of perceptual similarity are. On the other hand, knowledge is only slightly affected by even strong emotions, because procedural measurements are such.

The difference between notions and knowledge also manifests itself in dealing with contradictions. When contradiction arises, if notions are employed, then the contradiction is resolved by either omission of a premise or by stretching boundaries of some notions. On the other hand, if knowledge is employed, it forces one to search for false premises.

[124] *sukhamātyantikaṃ yattadbuddhigrāhyamatīndriyam* BhG 6.21.a

Whenever a judgment is generated by a vague sense of "it seems OK," or "it feels OK," or by a sense of emotional or cognitive dissonance, it is likely to be the result of a notion. In this case an appearance of certainty is derived from the strength of like/dislike attitudes.

Whenever a judgment is generated by a procedure, it is likely to be the result of a knowledge, and its certainty is derived from the degree of universality of that procedure.

Thinking with notions is guided by avoidance of cognitive and emotional dissonance. Thinking with knowledge is directed by logic and procedures.

Generalizations, induction, verbal formulations, and extrapolations usually lead to notions. In order to elevate a notion to the level of knowledge, it must be augmented with a procedure having definite conditions of applicability. This means that all definitions given here will, under the best circumstances, give rise to notions; these notions might be transformed into knowledge by practical application aimed at making them procedural.

Buddhi is "colored" by the three *guṇa*-s. *Rajas* guides the manipulation of knowledge; it is manifest in the process of deduction. *Tamas* provides for recognition of fragments of the perceptual stream as compatible with certain knowledge. *Sattva* facilitates forming new knowledge.

ahaṃkāra the faculty of relating everything to "self"; the faculty of maintaining persistence of "I."

Ahaṃkāra is "colored" by the three *guṇa*-s. *Rajas* enables changes to personal boundaries; *tamas* is instrumental in maintaining "the unchangeable core of self"; *sattva* enables self-investigation and self-knowledge.

Ordinarily, *ahaṃkāra* is present in the waking state of mind the same way the nose is present in the field of visual perception. The nose provides a reference that defines some of the interpretation of visual stimuli. The same way, *ahaṃkāra* is present in the back of the mind and makes perception, thoughts and actions referenced to personal constructs (it makes them into *vikalpa*-s).

antaḥkaraṇa (lit. "the inner instrument,") is the triad of *buddhi*, *ahaṃkāra* and *manas*. All components of the triad are are "colored" by the three *guṇa*-s: *sattva*, *rajas* or *tamas*.

jñānendriya qualities encompassing all perceptual features provided by sense organs: colors, pitch of sound, temperature, loudness, etc.
There are five types of *jñānendriya*-s provided by the faculties of vision, hearing, taste, smell and by the somatosensory system.

buddhīndriya = *jñānendriya*

mala fault-causing condition (lit. impurity).

It is a persistent configuration of *tattva*-s. It is a mental construct of a special kind that masks, inhibits, or outweighs other potentially active structures.

Three types of *mala*-s are defined: *āṇavamala*, *māyīyamala*, and *kārmamala*. Behind all types of *mala*-s is the *māyāśakti*.

The *āṇavamala*, being an evolute of *icchā-śakti*, has the nature of willful self-restriction.

The commentary to *sūtra* 9 of *Pratyabhijñāhṛdayam* states that *icchāśakti*, manifesting as an unobstructed self-will, when abridged and virtualized, turns into *āṇavamala*, manifesting itself as the sense of otherness and the lack of self-sufficiency.[125]

An *āṇavamala* manifests itself as a strong bias towards well defined borders between the concepts of "I" and "Not-Me." These borders are created by activation of aversions, preferences, and affections. An *āṇavamala* is not, per se, a preference of one alternative over another, but rather a *relish* of such preference. When such relish is augmented by *rāga-tattva*, it turns into an addiction to impose such preferences.

The relinquishment of the freedom of will while fully aware, and the lack of full awareness while following

[125] *apratihatasvātantryarūpā icchāśaktiḥ saṃkucitāsatī apūrṇamanyatārūpamāṇavaṃmalam*

one's own will — this is the twofold *āṇavamala*, twofold in the ways it impairs one's true character.[126]

When *āṇavamala* is present, logic is seen as devoid of a reflection of self, and thus, a knowledge bears that emptiness which is as if devoid of "self." So, *kārmamala* tends to be illogical, or even irrational, because of the resolve to manifest the fullness-of-self in opposition to the pure and full awareness.

A sense of powerlessness or lack of freedom, when a logical and consistent schema of a situation sinks in, comes from a forceful assertion of one's own prior resolutions. Those resolutions by virtue of one's addiction to them (that is, they are augmented with *rāga-tattva*), come into contradiction with the reality ("reality" is defined here as that part of perceptual space which is most independent of the tides of desires).

The *āṇavamala* is the root cause of two other types of *mala*-s.

The *māyīyamala* is a fragmentation of experiencing that inhibits the expression of freedom of will and restricts the freedom to act.

As stated in the commentary to the 9th *sūtra* of *Pratyabhijñāhṛdayam*, *jñānaśaktiḥ*, at reaching the state of directly experiencing something particular — gradually, beginning with contraction and moving towards delimitation of the ability to experience everything that is there to experience, having been in the configurations of *buddhīndriya*-s and *antaḥkaraṇa* — through locking into excessive abbreviation becomes *māyīyamala*, manifesting itself as a flow [of attention bias] into fragments of what is there to be experienced.[127]

One of the strongest expressions of the *māyīyamala* is the assumption that spoken words are true (and thus using them to guide further actions and analysis of a situation) when they are uttered by a figure one considers an authority or an *a priori* trusted source. To

---

[126] *svātantryahānir bodhasya svātantryasyāpy abodhatā* |
dvidhāṇavaṃ malam idaṃ svasvarūpāpahānitaḥ || K3.2.4

[127] *jñānaśaktiḥ krameṇasaṃkocādbhede sarvajñatvasya kiṃcijjñatvāpteḥ antaḥkaraṇabuddhīndriyatāpattipūrvamatyantasaṃkocagrahaṇena bhinnavedyaprathārūpaṃ māyīyaṃ malam*

counter the effects of *māyīyamala*, a functional assumption of the inherent indefiniteness of any perception is of great help (for example, ancient philosophers adhering to skepticism made the assumption of the indefiniteness; poker players make it too).

The *kārmamala* is constraining an action to a laced-with-personal-preferences script that impairs awareness.

As stated in the commentary to the 9th *sūtra* of *Pratyabhijñāhṛdayam*, *kriyāśakti*, at reaching the state of performing some definite action, constraining in stages the unlimited creativity and having assumed the configuration of *karmendriya*-s through locking into excessive abbreviation, arriving at an excessively encapsulated condition [becomes] *kārmamala*, consisting in acting in conformity with the effective/ineffective [axis][128]

Action, in its activation and structure, might be affected by other actions, by desires, by perceptions of inner and outer stimuli, and by knowledge. *kārmamala* is a restriction of such influences to actions and desires only. Just before an action is activated, the perceptive attention is inhibited or masked, allowing only other actions and desires to shape the current action, and making one as if momentarily blind.

mati procedural knowledge;
mental gesture;
functional attitude;
resolve.

mati is a non-verbal knowledge that is, at the same time, a continuous action.

dhāraṇa a persistent concentration of the mind upon something.

Yoga Sutra defines this term as "directing mind to one place."[129] Here is a script for practicing *dhāraṇa*:

1. Choose a spot in a perceptual field (e.g., a symbol on a uniform background);

---

[128] *kriyāśaktiḥ krameṇa bhede sarvakartṛtvasya kiṃcitkartṛtvāpteḥ karmendriyarūpasaṃkocagrahaṇapūrvaṃ atyantaparimitatāṃ prāptā śubhāśubhānuṣṭhānamayaṃ kārmaṃ malam*

[129] YS.3.1 *deśabandhaścittasyadhāraṇā*

2. Direct all of the attention to that spot;
3. When distraction occurs, simply return the focus of attention to that spot;
4. Keep doing 2 and 3 for at least 20 minutes.

dhyāna meditation. It is defined thus in Yoga Sutra[130] and in verse 146:[131]

It is a state of *buddhi* in the context of strong concentration of attention in which *buddhi*:

a. is steady, invariable, unchangeable;

b. has a single concept, or knowledge, that is not supported or conditioned by anything else present in short-term memory (that is, not conditioned by other concepts, by a percept, by an idea, by action, by wish, by desire, etc.);

c. directs attention of the senses, *manas*, and *ahaṃkāra* onto one object only; this concentration of attention does not result in less awareness;[132]

d. makes the flow of stimuli coalesce with that one object (*ekatānatā*).

For practical techniques of meditation, see [Ram98].

Meditation is not contemplation. During meditation there is no arrangement of thoughts; there is no intention to get somewhere, or to find a solution or an answer.

Hypnotic trance is related to meditation but is in many ways opposite to it. A big difference between the two is in reactivity to speech. In hypnotic trance, speech is automatically relevant to one's self, and some speech attains the power of an imperative. In meditation, speech is just a sound that has no immediate meaning or power to control. It passes through as if one is no

[130] YS.3.2. *tatra pratyayaikatānatā dhyānam*

[131] *dhyānaṃ hi niścalā buddhirnirākārā nirāśrayā*

[132] The degree of awareness might be known after the meditation by the degree one is able to recollect everything that was going on at the time of the meditation.

different from the surrounding air — without resistance and without attraction to it.

Another big difference is that the scope of awareness during hypnosis becomes narrow and focused, while in meditation it becomes broader and indefinite.

Yet another difference is in the direction and intensity of predominant flows of *vāyu*-s. During both states the flows are primarily through *iḍā* and *piṅgalā*. In meditation, the controlling flows are from *viśuddha-cakra* downwards, while in hypnosis, the controlling flows are from *mūladhāra-cakra* upwards. In meditation, the flows are less intense than in the hypnotic state.

samādhi the state of absorption that is defined thus in YS.3.3: That same *dhyāna*, when the object, that attention is directed to, is as if devoid of it's own substance or of unchangeable characteristics, is *samādhi.*[133]

The definition of *samādhi*, given in verses 6,7, and 8 of HYP.4, is on three planes: the gross, the subtle and the ultimate, correspondingly.

As salt dissolves in the waters of the sea without a trace, so a homologous unity between the breath and *manas* is realized as *samādhi.*[134]

When *prāṇa* is depleted and all fabrications by *manas* dissolve, then the self-sameness of the sentiment is realized as *samādhi.*[135]

The identity between the [limited] individual and the ultimate "Self" [that has assumed that limited configuration, which is perceived as an individual], the equality between the two — the state in which all notions, formed in the mind due to volition, vanish — is realized as *samādhi.*[136]

---

[133] *tadevārthamātranirbhāsaṃ svarūpaśūnyamiva samādhiḥ*

[134] *salile saindhavaṃ yadvatsāmyaṃ bhajati yogataḥ* |
tathātmamanasorikyaṃ samādhirabhidhīyate || HYP.4.5

[135] *yadā saṃkṣīyate prāṇo mānasaṃ ca pralīyate* |
tadā samarasatvaṃ ca samādhirabhidhīyate ||

[136] *tatsamaṃ ca dvayoraikyaṃ jīvātmaparamātmanoḥ* |
praṇaṣṭasarvasaṅkalpaḥ samādhiḥ so'bhidhīyate ||

Appendix

Location of Chakras

(all chakras are shown 1.5x normal size; lower six are the size of a thumb width)

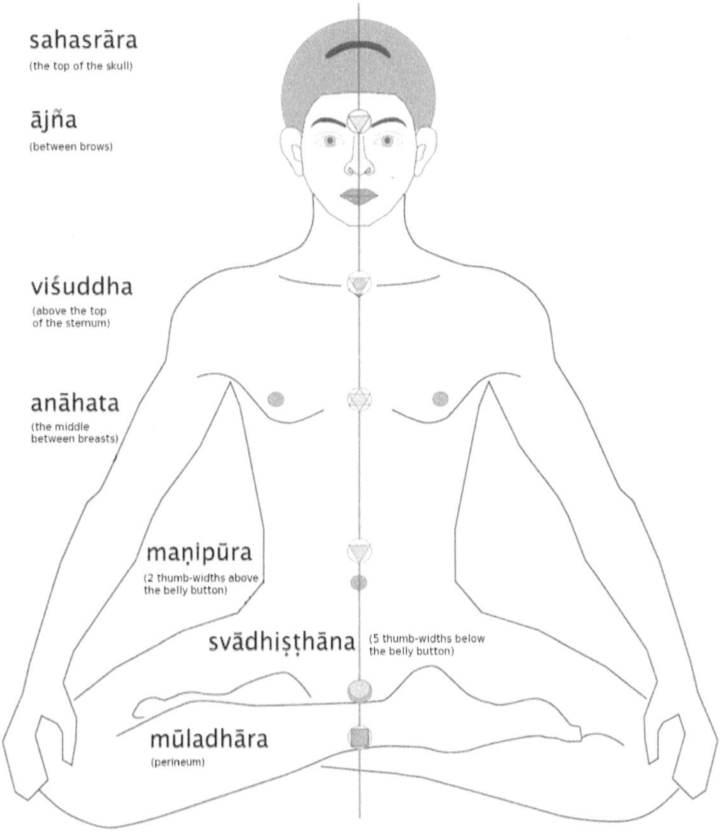

Bibliography

[Cou01] H. David Coulter. *Anatomy of Hatha Yoga.* Body and Breath, 2001.

[Iye99] B.K.S. Iyengar. *Light on Pranayama.* The Crossroad Publishing Company, 1999.

[Joo02] Swami Lakshman Joo. *Vijnana Bhairava, The Practice of Centering Awareness.* Indica Books, 2002.

[Kah98] Eivind Kahrs. *Indian semantic analysis, The 'nirvacana' tradition.* Cambridge University Press, 1998.

[Lak00] Swami Lakshmanjoo. *Kashmir Shaivism, The Secret Supreme.* Kashmir Shaivism Fellowship, 2000.

[LR08] Ph.D. Lorin Roche. *The Radiance Sutras.* Syzygy Creations, 2008.

[Odi05] Daniel Odier. *Yoga Spandakarika.* Inner Traditions, 2005.

[Osh94] Osho. *The Book of Secrets.* St.Martin's Griffin, 1994.

[Ram82] Swami Rama. *Enlightment without God.* The Himalayan International Institute of Yoga Science and Philosophy of thew U.S.A., 1982.

[Ram96] Swami Rama. *Path of Fire and Light Vol.2.* The Himalayan Institute Press, 1996.

[Ram98] Swami Rama. *Meditation and Its Practice.* The Himalayan Institute Press, 1998.

[Sar03] Swami Satyasangananda Saraswati. *Sri Vijnana Bhairava Tantra, The Ascent.* Yoga Publications Trust, 2003.

[Sem08] Dmitri Semenov. *The Essence of Self-Recognition.* Sattarka Publications, 2008.

[Sin00] Jaideva Singh. *Shiva Sutras. The Yoga of Supreme Identity.* Motilal Banarsidass, 2000.

[Sin03a] Jaideva Singh. *The Secret of Self Recognition.* Motilal Banarsidass, 2003.

[Sin03b] Jaideva Singh. *Vijnanabhairava or Divine Consciousness.* Motilal Banarsidass, 2003.

[SR98] Alan Hymes Swami Rama, Rudolph Bellentine. *Science of Breath.* The Himalayan Institute Press, 1998.

[Tor02] Raffaele Torella. *Ishvarapratyabhijnakarika of Utpaladeva with the Authors's Vritti.* Motilal Banarsidass, 2002.

Index

ājña-cakra, 45, 67, **191**
ānandaśakti, **172**
ahaṃkāra, **185**, 189
anāhata-cakra, 30, 40, 45, 46, 54, 58, 65, 67, **191**
antaḥkaraṇa, **186**
apāna, 29, 58, 77, 129, 158, 163, 174, **175**, 177
buddhi, 67, 151, 179, **184**, 189
buddhīndriya, **186**
cakra, 35, 61, 78, 90, 91, **175**, 191
camatkāra, **171**
cicchakti, **172**
cit, **171**
dhāraṇa, 10, 141, **188**
dhyāna, 141, **189**, 190
guṇa, **183**
icchāśakti, **172**
iḍā, 190
jñānendriya, **186**
jñānaśakti, **172**
kāla-tattva, 109, **180**, 181
kalā, 109, **178**, 180
kalā-tattva, 109, **178**, 181
kañcuka, 178, **181**
karma, **177**, 179
kriyāśakti, **172**
māyā, **178**
mahābhūta, 71, 174, **182**
mala, **186**
manas, 29, 39, 40, 42, 59, 60, 69, 112, 123, 130, 144, 147, 159, **183**, 184, 186, 189, 190
mati, 136, 140, 141, 146, 159, **188**
mūladhāra-cakra, 34, 35, 53, 54, 190, **191**
nāḍī, **175**
niyati-tattva, 109, **180**, 181
piṅgalā, 190
prāṇa, 29, 58, 77, 80, 81, 87, 158, 163, 174, **175**, 177, 190
prājña, 67
prakāśa, **170**
pramātṛ, 179
rāga-tattva, 109, **179**, 181
rajas, **183**
samādhi, 174, **190**
sattva, **183**
śakti, 27
śakti, 17, 18, 20, 21, 23–29, 32–35, 39, 41, 43, 47, 53, 63, 88, 90, 118, 169, **172**
śiva, 17, 18, 25, 26, 43, 44, 51, 94, 114, 124, 136, 146, 162, 169, **171**
svātantrya, **171**
taijasa, 67
tamas, **183**
tattva, 13, 63, 69, 70, 74, 79, 90, 100, 109, 113, 117, 151, **172**, 178, 181, 186
vāyu, **174**, 175, 190

vaiśvānara, 67
vidyā-tattva, 109, **179**, 181
vikalpa, 55, 56, 76, 108, 123, 130, 138, 159, **176**
vimarśa, **171**
viśuddha-cakra, 67, 190, **191**

www.ingramcontent.com/pod-product-compliance
Lightning Source LLC
Chambersburg PA
CBHW022009160426
43197CB00007B/349
9780578060422